EYEWITNESS
GANDHI

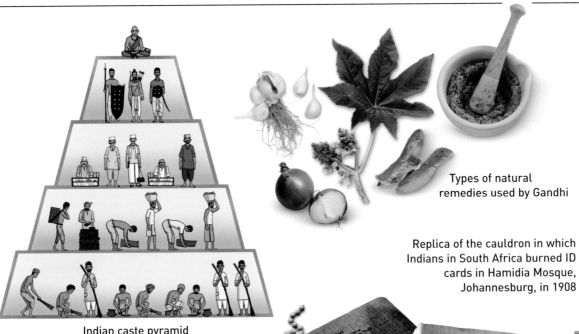

Indian caste pyramid

Types of natural remedies used by Gandhi

Replica of the cauldron in which Indians in South Africa burned ID cards in Hamidia Mosque, Johannesburg, in 1908

Prayer beads

Gandhi's eyeglasses

Gandhi's autobiography, *The Story of My Experiments with Truth*

Gandhi as a lawyer in London

Boer War medal

Coat of arms of the English East India Company

Gandhi Memorial in Gandhi Smriti, New Delhi

Three wise monkeys, epitomizing Gandhi's ideals

Poster carrying an appeal
to buy Indian paper, 1940

EYEWITNESS
GANDHI

Written by
JUHI SAKLANI

Consultant
VIVEK BHANDARI

Bowl and plate
used by Gandhi

Example of the type of spinning wheel
used by Gandhi

Raw indigo dye
extracted from
Indigofera tinctoria plant

LONDON, NEW YORK,
MELBOURNE, MUNICH, and DELHI

Senior editor Dipali Singh
Editor Medha Gupta
Designers Astha Singh, Sukriti Sobti
Picture researcher Sakshi Saluja
Picture research manager Taiyaba Khatoon
Senior cartographer Swati Handoo
Cartography manager Suresh Kumar
Managing editor Alka Ranjan
Managing art editor Romi Chakraborty
DTP designers Nandkishor Acharya,
Ganesh Sharma, Jagtar Singh
Senior producer Charlotte Cade
Print programme manager Luca Frassinetti
Managing director Aparna Sharma

First American Edition, 2014
Published in the United States by
DK Publishing
4th floor, 345 Hudson Street
New York, New York 10014

14 15 16 17 18 10 9 8 7 6 5 4 3 2
257057—09/14

Copyright © 2014 Dorling Kindersley Limited

Published in Great Britain by Dorling Kindersley Limited.

A catalog record for this book is available from the Library of Congress.
ISBN: 978-1-4654-2684-0 (Paperback)
ISBN: 978-1-4654-2698-7 (ALB)

DK books are available at special discounts when purchased in bulk
for sales promotions, premiums, fund-raising, or educational use.
For details, contact: DK Publishing Special Markets, 345 Hudson Street,
New York, New York 10014 or SpecialSales@dk.com.

Printed and bound in China by South China Printing Co. Ltd.

Discover more at
www.dk.com

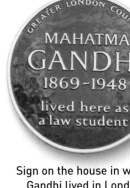

Sign on the house in which
Gandhi lived in London

Sri Mahadevar
Temple, Vaikom,
Kerala

Gandhi in
Noakhali, East
Bengal (now in
Bangladesh)

Replicas of the type of *khadau*
(wooden sandals) worn by Gandhi

World Peace gong,
Gandhi Smriti, New Delhi

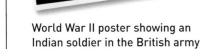

World War II poster showing an
Indian soldier in the British army

Contents

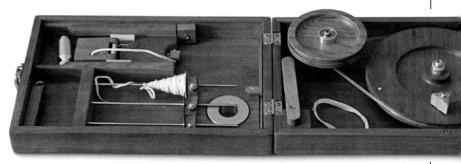

A portable *charkha* similar to the type used by Gandhi

Introducing Gandhi

Mohandas Karamchand Gandhi (October 2, 1869–January 30, 1948) was the inspirational political leader who led India to freedom from British colonial rule by adopting peaceful means of protest. Gandhi's commitment to the welfare of the poor, his efforts to bring harmony at all levels of society, and his personal asceticism earned him the title "Mahatma," or "great soul."

"My life is my message."

MAHATMA GANDHI

Coat of arms of Porbandar state

Product of his times

Gandhi was born in British India at a time during which Indians were considered inferior. Even his father, a minister in the princely state of Porbandar, did not receive the respect he deserved. Gandhi was aware of the problems within his own society as well, such as discrimination against people from lower castes (*see* p.27).

Three wise monkeys

Covering their eyes, ears, and mouth with their hands, the three wise monkeys "see no evil, hear no evil, and speak no evil," epitomizing Gandhi's philosophy of truth and nonviolence. Given to Gandhi by visitors from China, these monkeys illustrate his idea of a truthful life.

Man of few possessions

The Mahatma was a deeply spiritual man who did not get distracted by worldly possessions or power. Identifying with India's poor, he lived very simply and only wore a handwoven *dhoti*, or loincloth. His pair of eyeglasses, pen, prayer book, spinning wheel, and wooden sandals were among his few personal belongings.

India's leader of the masses

Gandhi converted the Indian freedom movement from a narrow struggle of lawyers and politicians into a mass uprising. After working for the rights of Indians living in South Africa, Gandhi inspired millions in his own country to fight against the British rule without hatred or violence. Gandhi's *satyagraha,* or truth-force (*see* p.16), galvanized millions of Indians to face police brutalities with a dignity that impressed the world.

Gandhi wore simple clothes to identify with ordinary Indians in South Africa

Gandhi in London to attend the Second Round Table Conference, 1931

Truly global

Gandhi took the world's best ideas and applied them to India. Educated in London, he became an activist in South Africa and learned from thinkers such as Henry David Thoreau, Leo Tolstoy, and John Ruskin. In turn, he inspired leaders like Martin Luther King, Jr., Nelson Mandela, and Barack Obama.

British Empire

From the 15th to the 18th century, Europeans explored the world by sea in search of new trade routes. Countries such as Portugal, Spain, Britain, and France conquered territories and established colonies in the Americas, Africa, Asia, and Australia, bringing much of the world under their rule. Britain soon asserted its dominance with its superior gunpower, strong navy, and diplomacy, and created the mighty British Empire.

NORTH AMERICA

PACIFIC OCEAN

Trading empires

Between the late 15th and 18th centuries, the Portuguese and Dutch, followed by the British, developed large trading empires stretching to Africa, Asia, the Americas, and Australia. By the 17th century, the English East India Company, a merchant company, had gained a foothold in India by establishing Fort St. George (in southern India)—an important port and entry point to India.

Industrial Revolution

Abundant raw materials, available capital, and key technological developments, such as the steam engine, created conditions ripe for an industrial revolution in Britain. Invented by Thomas Newcomen in 1712, the steam engine was improved by James Watt. It replaced the water wheel and horses—which were slow and unreliable—as the main source of power for British industry, contributing to large-scale production and faster transportation by steamships and railroads.

Slave chains

Slave trade

Flexible ways of financing sea voyages gave fresh impetus to Britain's slave trade. By the 1780s, British ships were carrying 40,000 slaves from Africa to the Americas annually. Trinkets, textiles, and weapons were sent to Africa and exchanged for slaves, who were sold for huge profit in the Americas.

Model of James Watt's steam engine, which paved the way for the Industrial Revolution

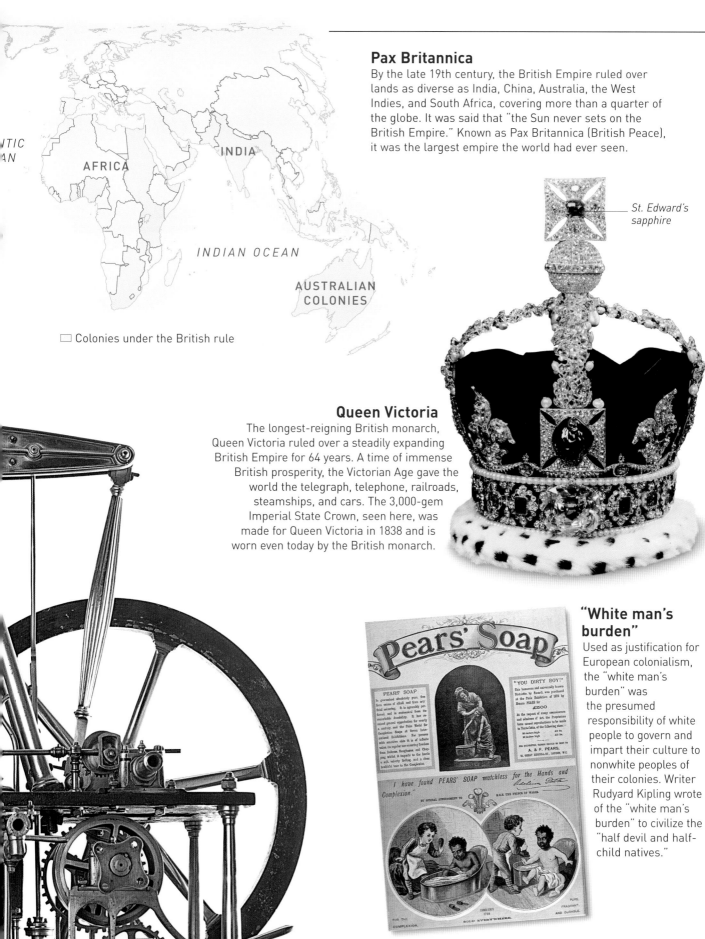

Pax Britannica

By the late 19th century, the British Empire ruled over lands as diverse as India, China, Australia, the West Indies, and South Africa, covering more than a quarter of the globe. It was said that "the Sun never sets on the British Empire." Known as Pax Britannica (British Peace), it was the largest empire the world had ever seen.

AFRICA

INDIA

INDIAN OCEAN

AUSTRALIAN COLONIES

☐ Colonies under the British rule

St. Edward's sapphire

Queen Victoria

The longest-reigning British monarch, Queen Victoria ruled over a steadily expanding British Empire for 64 years. A time of immense British prosperity, the Victorian Age gave the world the telegraph, telephone, railroads, steamships, and cars. The 3,000-gem Imperial State Crown, seen here, was made for Queen Victoria in 1838 and is worn even today by the British monarch.

"White man's burden"

Used as justification for European colonialism, the "white man's burden" was the presumed responsibility of white people to govern and impart their culture to nonwhite peoples of their colonies. Writer Rudyard Kipling wrote of the "white man's burden" to civilize the "half devil and half-child natives."

Pears' Soap advertisement likening light skin color to cleanliness and racial superiority, 1880

Mohandas, age seven, posing for a studio photograph

Early years
(1869–87)

Mohandas Karamchand Gandhi was born on October 2, 1869, in Porbandar, a seaside town in the province of Gujarat. He grew up in British India, in the princely states of Porbandar and Rajkot. A shy and physically weak boy, Mohandas hardly seemed like a person who would challenge the British Empire 50 years later. However, this truth-loving child showed many signs of becoming a "Mahatma," or "great soul."

In the family
Karamchand, Mohandas's father, served as the prime minister of the Porbandar and Rajkot princely states. Liberal for his times, Karamchand had friends from all religions. Mohandas's mother, Putlibai, was a pious woman who regularly visited temples and observed rigorous fasts.

Childhood memories
Lovingly called "Monia," Mohandas was his parents' youngest child. Often getting into mischief, he and his friends once tried to steal a statue from a temple, but were caught by the priest. While his friends denied any part in the prank, six-year-old Mohandas owned up to it.

"The outstanding impression my mother has left on my memory is that of saintliness. She was deeply religious."

MAHATMA GANDHI
In his autobiography, *The Story of My Experiments with Truth*, 1927

Gandhi's father, Karamchand, and mother, Putlibai

Early marriage

In keeping with the norms of the time, Mohandas was married to Kastur Kapadia at the age of 13. She was also 13. While the young husband wanted to educate his illiterate wife, an opinionated Kastur refused to be taught by him, preferring to play with her friends.

A much older Gandhi and his wife, Kastur, 1915

School years

An average but diligent student, Mohandas studied at Alfred High School in Rajkot. During a school examination, he misspelled the word "kettle" and was prompted by his teacher to copy the word from another student. But the honest boy refused to do so.

A Raja Ravi Varma painting showing a scene from King Harishchandra's story

Finding a hero

Hindu mythological tales left a deep impression on Mohandas. A lasting influence was King Harishchandra's story, which he saw in a play. Moved by the king's sacrifice of his kingdom and family to follow the path of truth, Mohandas resolved always to be truthful.

A Hindu Brahmin wearing *janeu*

Nonvegetarian thali *(platter)*

Janeu *(sacred thread)*

Experiments with eating meat

As Vaishnava Hindus, the Gandhis were strict vegetarians. Urged by a friend to try eating meat, Mohandas ate it on the sly to gain strength to "defeat the British." Unable to lie for long, he soon gave up the experiment.

Sacred thread

Brahmins (see p. 27)—the highest caste in Indian social hierarchy—wear *janeu*, or sacred thread. Mohandas belonged to the lower Bania caste and envied the Brahmins sporting their threads and wanted one for himself. This boy would go on to reform the Indian caste system.

Mohandas in London
(1888–91)

At the age of 19, Mohandas Gandhi went to London to study law. To do so, he had to surmount a number of hurdles before his journey. Religious rules of the time forbade Hindus from traveling abroad. Also, his family fiercely opposed the idea of him living in a foreign country. His mother finally gave in when he took an oath of abstinence from meat, wine, and female companions. Mohandas sailed to England in 1888, the first person from his community to go overseas.

English gentleman
To fit into British society, Mohandas enrolled in dance, violin, and English elocution classes. He dressed as a fashionable Englishman, wearing a stylish jacket, a silk shirt, and a bow tie. Later in life, he would call this phase an "infatuation" that lasted three months.

Living the London dream
Mohandas arrived in England in September 1888. Home to thinkers and philosophers, 19th-century London was stirring with ideas of socialism, women's rights, and universal religion, inspiring young Gandhi to form his own views on different issues.

Big Ben and Westminster Palace, 19th-century London

After reading a book on vegetarianism, Gandhi became an active member of the London Vegetarian Society.

Young Gandhi with other members of the Vegetarian Society at a conference in Portsmouth, England, 1891

Sign outside the house in which Gandhi lived in London

Spiritual journey

While in London, Gandhi met theosophists Madame Blavatsky and Annie Besant, who believed in the pursuit of truth and universal brotherhood. He read Blavatsky's book, *Key to Theosophy*, which gave him a sense of the theosophists' respect for Hinduisim and inspired him to read the *Bhagavad Gita*, an ancient Hindu scripture.

Simple life

Aware that his older brother had funded his stay in London, Mohandas adopted a simple lifestyle to reduce his expenses. He lived in inexpensive housing, cooked his own food, and often walked long distances to save money on transportation.

Learning law

In Mohandas's time, passing law school exams by "cramming" and relying on study guides was the norm. Gandhi, however, felt "it was a fraud... not to read these books." He even learned Latin to read original legal texts. He earned his law degree from the Inner Temple, London, on June 10, 1891.

Diploma awarded to Gandhi

In South Africa

In 1893, Gandhi went to South Africa to assist an Indian firm in a legal case. At the time, South Africa was divided into British and Boer, or Dutch, colonies. Indians lived in the country as traders and laborers and were systematically discriminated against. Gandhi, a victim of racial bias himself, decided to stay on and help the Indians in South Africa in the fight for their rights.

Late 19th-century Southern Africa

South Africa was not a unified country when Gandhi arrived. It consisted of four provinces populated by native peoples, such as the Zulu and Xhosa, but ruled by Europeans. Natal was a British colony, the Cape was a self-ruling British province, and the Transvaal and Orange Free State were independent Boer republics.

□ Boer-ruled states
□ Self-ruling British state
□ British colony
□ British protectorate

Model depicting the Pietermaritzburg incident

Not first class at all!

Gandhi was traveling in a first-class train car from Natal to Durban to attend court. At Pietermaritzburg, he was asked to leave the train by white passengers who objected to a "colored" person traveling with them. Gandhi refused, but he was thrown out of his compartment by a policeman. The incident inspired him to stay in South Africa and fight against racism.

Indians or coolies?

Many Indians went to South Africa as "indentured labor," bound by an agreement to serve their employers in plantations abroad or at home. Most were Tamil- or Telugu-speaking people from southern India. Europeans contemptuously called them "coolies" or "samis," a corruption of "Swami," a common Tamil last name.

The £3 ($15) tax certificate issued to Indians in South Africa

1874, Natal tried to introduce a £2.5 ($10) tax on indentured Indians, who could not afford it.

From lawyer to activist

In 1894, Natal, where Gandhi lived, proposed a law to deny Indians the right to vote. Gandhi canceled his plans to return to India and helped Indians in South Africa organize protests against this injustice. Through petitions and press propaganda, they made their voices heard and united Indians in South Africa.

Natal Indian Congress

To promote the campaign for Indian rights, Gandhi and his colleagues formed the Natal Indian Congress on May 22, 1894. Gandhi explained its goals in two pamphlets, *An Appeal to Every Briton in South Africa* and *The Indian Franchise: An Appeal*. Eventually, awareness about the Indians' plight began to spread.

Gandhi's statue at Government Square, renamed Gandhi Square, Johannesburg, South Africa

Green Pamphlet and its fallout

During his visit to India in 1896, Gandhi wrote the "Green Pamphlet" (named for its green cover), bringing attention to the prejudice faced by Indians in South Africa. Widely publicized, it incited a white mob to try and lynch Gandhi when he returned to Durban. Pelted with stones and eggs, he escaped with the help of local police.

Boer War medal

Satyagraha begins

Between 1903 and 1914, Gandhi launched and developed *satyagraha*, or truth-force, to protest unjust laws imposed on Indians in South Africa. *Satyagraha* is a philosophy of peaceful protest in which the protester remains nonviolent, despite provocation. Thousands of Indians responded to Gandhi by disobeying laws and courting arrest peaceably, especially in the Transvaal, which had become a British colony after the Boer War in 1902.

Ambulance corps

During the Anglo-Boer War (1899–1902), fought between the British and Dutch settlers in South Africa, Gandhi raised an ambulance corps to provide medical aid for wounded British soldiers. He felt that this show of loyalty toward the Empire would ensure equal rights for Indians in South Africa. Gandhi was awarded a medal for his services. He provided similar services during the Zulu Rebellion in 1906.

Indian Opinion is born

A journal called *Indian Opinion* was launched in 1903 in Durban with Gandhi's support. Published in four languages— English, Hindi, Tamil, and Gujarati— it became the Indian voice in South Africa. Because of financial pressures, in 1904, Gandhi moved the offices from Durban to Phoenix, a rural settlement outside Durban.

First edition of *Indian Opinion*, 1903

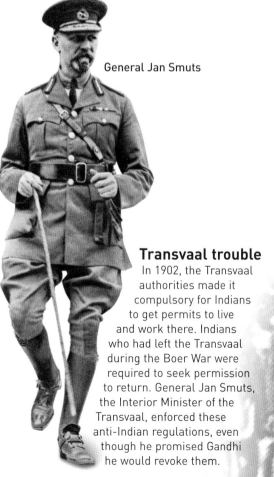

General Jan Smuts

Transvaal trouble

In 1902, the Transvaal authorities made it compulsory for Indians to get permits to live and work there. Indians who had left the Transvaal during the Boer War were required to seek permission to return. General Jan Smuts, the Interior Minister of the Transvaal, enforced these anti-Indian regulations, even though he promised Gandhi he would revoke them.

drew media attention.

Gandhi's original Transvaal Asiatic Registration Certificate

Replica of the cauldron, commemorating the 1908 protest, Hamidia Mosque, Johannesburg

Drama in two acts

In 1907, Gandhi led a mass protest against two unfair anti-Indian acts passed by Transvaal authorities. These acts made it compulsory for Indians to register with the authorities, be fingerprinted, and carry registration certificates. It also denied entry to new Indians into the state.

Great March

In 1913, Transvaal authorities declared non-Christian marriages illegal. In addition, they began levying a £3 ($15) tax on Indian contract laborers. In protest, Gandhi initiated a *satyagraha*. More than 2,000 Indians took to the streets in protest, and workers went on strike. On March 7, 1914, the Indian Relief Act abolished the tax and legalized marriages performed according to Indian customs.

World influences

"I have humbly endeavored to follow Tolstoy, Ruskin, Thoreau, Emerson, and other writers, besides the masters of Indian philosophy," said Gandhi in his book *Hind Swaraj*. He valued Western intellectuals. Indeed, many influences on his work came from philosophers and writers from all over the world. Gandhi merged their ideas with his own understanding of life.

Suffragette Movement

When Gandhi visited England in 1906, the streets were packed with women demanding an equal right to vote, or suffrage. Admiring their courageous methods of protest, he urged the Indians of South Africa to learn from these women who were unafraid to go to prison.

Emmeline Pankhurst, leader of the Suffragette Movement, being arrested on May 21, 1914

Romain Rolland

Gandhi always corresponded with people from other countries, including the French writer and Nobel Prize winner Romain Rolland (1866–1944), who kept Gandhi in touch with developments in Europe. Deeply critical of imperialism, he was influenced by Gandhi's philosophy of nonviolence. In 1924, Rolland wrote a short biography of Gandhi.

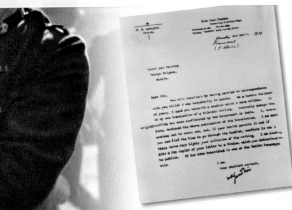

Thoreau advocated a life close to nature and lived in this house near Walden Pond, Massachusetts

Leo Tolstoy

The writer of literary classics such as *War and Peace* and *Anna Karenina*, the Russian novelist Leo Tolstoy (1878–1910) inspired Gandhi with his religious-philosophical work *The Kingdom of God is Within You*, in which Tolstoy asked people to follow the teachings of Jesus Christ. The two men corresponded with each other through letters.

John Ruskin

The British thinker who affected Gandhi most profoundly was John Ruskin (1819–1900). Stirred by Ruskin's book *Unto This Last*, Gandhi decided to put its principles into practice right away. He started the Phoenix farm in South Africa, where all people were considered equal and the same value was attached to all work, whether intellectual or menial.

St. Matthew's portrait in Old Trinity Church, Massachusetts

Lord Krishna

Arjuna

Spiritual influences

Gandhi often cited the *Bhagavad Gita*, a Hindu religious poem, part of the epic *Mahabharata*, and the "Sermon on the Mount" in the Bible among his spiritual influences. While the former carries Lord Krishna's teachings about selfless action, the latter contains Jesus Christ's lessons on love and compassion.

A scene from the *Mahabharata* showing Lord Krishna sermonizing Arjuna, the warrior prince, about selfless action, which formed the basis for the *Bhagavad Gita*

Portrail of the Raj

English EIC coat of arms

English East India Company

The Mogul Emperor Jehangir gave the Company concessions to trade in India, allowing it to gain a vital foothold in the country. Later, the English EIC sought and received permission to collect taxes, build forts, raise an army, and mint its own currency. By 1833, the Company was ruling most of India in the name of the British Crown.

In 1600, the British Crown gave the English East India Company (EIC) the sole right to trade with India. The profits were so huge that the Company fought battles with the French, Dutch, and Portuguese to gain control over the subcontinent. By 1857, the Mogul Empire had weakened, and the British Crown began direct rule over India, a phase in history known as the British Raj.

Economics and the Raj

The British made the Indian farmers grow cash crops, such as cotton, which they bought at cheap rates and sold at a profit. They did not allow local industries to develop, forcing Indians to buy finished goods imported from Britain.

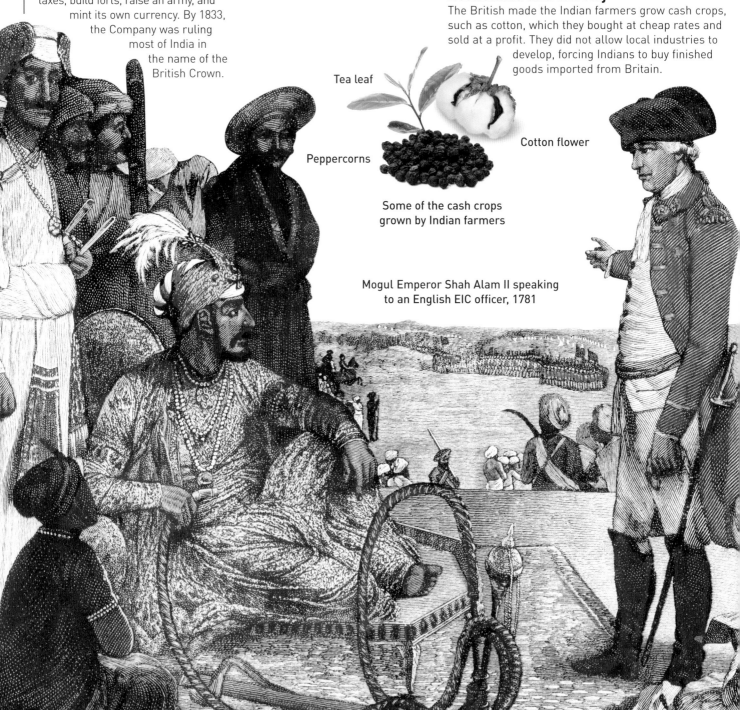

Tea leaf

Peppercorns

Cotton flower

Some of the cash crops grown by Indian farmers

Mogul Emperor Shah Alam II speaking to an English EIC officer, 1781

Revolt of 1857

The Indian soldiers of the Company were unhappy about the racial discrimination they faced in the army and the unjust takeovers of some princely states, such as Awadh and Jhansi. When asked to bite open cartridges greased with beef and pork fat, which was against their religious beliefs, they finally revolted. The revolt was brutally crushed by British forces.

Princely states

Even as the British ruled India, there existed nearly 565 kingdoms, or princely states, such as Mysore and Baroda, in India. The rulers of these kingdoms helped the British collect revenue and offered them military help. In return, they enjoyed nominal powers, received titles, and amassed huge personal wealth.

Stamp featuring Maharaja Sir Ganga Singh, ruler of Bikaner, a princely state

Doubting Thomas

Thomas Babington Macaulay, a British official, argued to replace Persian and Sanskrit with English as the medium of instruction in Indian schools. He wanted Indians to learn modern ideas and adopt Western ways. Ignorant of Indian civilization, he maintained that European knowledge was superior.

Manufactured in 1855, the *Fairy Queen* survives as the world's oldest working railroad engine

Advent of modern technology

Technological innovations in the late 19th century united Indians like never before. While railroads connected the country, the press brought information from all over India. Educated and committed Indians came together to form the Indian National Congress, the party that later spearheaded the freedom struggle.

Hind Swaraj

Gandhi wrote the book *Hind Swaraj* (Indian Home Rule) in 1909. Penned in Gujarati and later translated into English, it was written in 10 days, while Gandhi sailed on a ship from England to South Africa. Composed in a dialogue form between the "Editor" and the "Reader," the book spoke about how to challenge British rule in India. It tried to spread the idea of nonviolence among Indians.

Tolstoy's letter
The Russian writer Leo Tolstoy wrote "A Letter to a Hindoo" in 1908, urging Indians to refuse cooperation with the British, but without indulging in violence. Tolstoy's ideas inspired Gandhi to write *Hind Swaraj.*

Statue of Leo Tolstoy, Doukhobor Museum, Canada

Is civilization civilized?
In *Hind Swaraj*, Gandhi criticized a Western civilization marked by greed and temptation. He said that colonial empires were formed by gun power and motivated by the greed for luxury. India, he felt, should opt for simplicity; good conduct, not power; and nonviolence, not force.

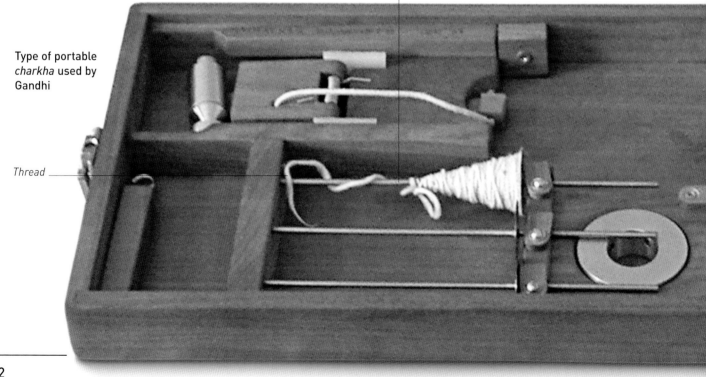

Spindle

Type of portable *charkha* used by Gandhi

Thread

ARABIAN
SEA ✷ Poona

BAY OF
BENGAL

Map of undivided
India, 1909

✷ Tinnevelly

☐ British India
☐ Native states and territories
✷ Cities facing violent protests

Cartoon showing
Gandhi protesting
in front of a tank,
symbolizing
British rule, 1930

Might is not right

Hind Swaraj laid down a clear moral
strategy for battling an oppressor. If
the British were ruling India because
of their military might, the answer
was not to fight back with firearms,
but to retaliate with the force of the
soul and a clear conscience.

Meaning of swaraj

Swaraj translates as "self-rule" or "home rule."
For Gandhi, it meant not only that the people of a
country should govern themselves freely, but also
that each person should examine his own faults to
be worthy of self-rule. He believed that if Indians
wanted freedom, they, too, had to stop treating
low-caste (*see* p.38) Indians as inferior people.

INDIAN
HOME RULE

BY

M. K. GANDHI

Being a Translation of "Hind Swaraj" (Indian
Home Rule), published in the Gujarati
columns of INDIAN OPINION,
11th and 18th Dec.,
1909

No Rights Reserved

THE INTERNATIONAL PRINTING PRESS
PHOENIX, NATAL
1910

Spinning a revolution

For Gandhi, a crucial aspect of
attaining *swaraj* was his refusal to use
British goods. He made the use of
swadeshi, or Indian, cloth a pillar of
India's freedom struggle. To help poor
weavers, he used a
charkha, or "spinning
wheel," daily to urge
Indians to use
swadeshi cloth.

Small wheel

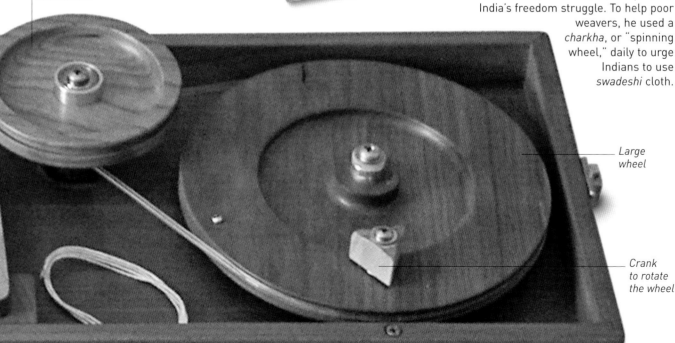

*Large
wheel*

*Crank
to rotate
the wheel*

Return to India

Gandhi returned to India from South Africa in 1915. India had become more politically active since he had left it in 1893. To involve ordinary people in the freedom struggle, Gandhi traveled extensively across India. His interventions in peasant matters won him respect, and people began calling him *Bapu*, or "father."

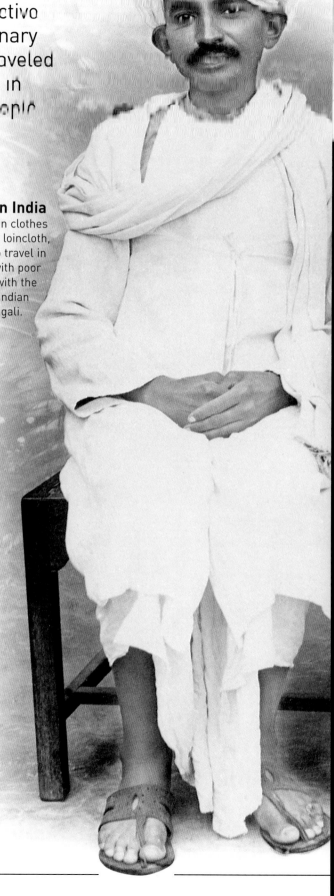

Indian in India
In India, Gandhi gave up European clothes and started wearing a *dhoti*, or loincloth, like everyday Indians. He chose to travel in third-class railroad cars with poor Indians. To connect better with the masses, he learned other Indian languages, such as Bengali.

Gopal Krishna Gokhale
An eminent leader in Congress, Gopal Krishna Gokhale (1866–1915) was Gandhi's political mentor. Impressed by Gokhale's ideals of public service, Gandhi followed his advice to travel in India to understand the plight of the common people.

Yarn dyed with indigo to color it blue

Raw indigo dye

Bapu in Bihar
In 1917, Gandhi visited Champaran in Bihar, in eastern India, where British landlords were forcing peasants to grow indigo instead of food crops, and to pay taxes in a time of famine. Gandhi mobilized the locals and courted arrest to draw attention to the cause. Eventually, the government stopped the forced cultivation and withdrew the unjust taxes.

Kheda satyagraha

Gandhi supported a peasant struggle in Gujarat's famine-hit Kheda district, where the government wanted to increase taxes on the locals. In 1918, the peasants refused to pay, which led to many arrests. They stood their ground, however, forcing the government to stop levying the tax.

Mahatma Gandhi with social workers in Kheda, Gujarat

"The Kheda satyagraha *marks the beginning of an awakening among the peasants of Gujarat, the beginning of their true political education."*

MAHATMA GANDHI
The Story of My Experiments with Truth, 1927

Star of India

World War I and India

Gandhi supported the British during World War I (1914–18), fought between the Allies (UK, France, and Russia) and the Central Powers (Germany, Austria-Hungary, and the Ottoman Empire). Gandhi believed in the fairness of the British and felt he could negotiate for better treatment of Indians in return for this show of loyalty.

Postcard showing various British colonies that participated in WWI

Names of Indian soldiers killed in WWI engraved on the podium

WWI memorial dedicated to Indian soldiers, Neuve Chapelle, France

Gandhi's ashrams

In 1904, on his way to Durban on a train from Johannesburg, Gandhi read John Ruskin's *Unto This Last*. Eager to put the book's message into practice, he founded a farm community in Phoenix, near Durban. Here, like-minded people led a simple life based on equality and dignity of labour. Determined to continue his experiments with community living after his return from South Africa, Gandhi set up ashrams, similar to Phoenix farm, in many Indian cities.

Replicas of the type of *khadau* (wooden sandals) worn by Gandhi

Tolstoy Farm
Faced with the huge task of helping the families of *satyagrahis*, or protesters, jailed for defying the anti-Indian law TARA (Transvaal Asiatic Registration Act), Gandhi set up the Tolstoy Farm near Johannesburg in 1910. Named after the Russian writer Leo Tolstoy, the farm welcomed people of all religious and social backgrounds.

Sabarmati Ashram
Founded on the banks of the Sabarmati River in Ahmedabad, Gujarat, in 1917, Sabarmati Ashram was the center of Gandhi's social and political work in India. Defining moments of the Indian freedom movement were conceived here. It was here that Gandhi began spinning the *charkha*, setting an example for Indians to make their own cloth.

Charkha, *"spinning wheel"*

Gandhi's walking stick

watch and eyeglasses.

Vaishyas, or the merchants and traders

Shudras, or the unskilled workers

Indian caste structure

The Indian caste system during Gandhi's time was hierarchical, in which Brahmins occupied the highest rung and the "untouchables" the lowest. When Gandhi admitted a couple belonging to the untouchable caste to Sabarmati Ashram, many members protested. Gandhi, however, stood his ground, and the couple slowly gained acceptance.

"Untouchables," or pariahs

Indian caste pyramid

The room where Gandhi lived, Sabarmati Ashram, Ahmedabad

Gandhi's writing table

Sevagram

Consisting of several small huts, Sevagram (Village of Service) in Maharashtra was the final ashram set up by Gandhi at the age of 67. Built in 1937 to serve the poor and untouchables, Sevagram also became an important center of India's political life.

Family and friends

"Whatever I am is because of her," said Gandhi of his wife, Kasturba. In addition to his wife and their four sons, he had a close circle of friends and disciples who were immensely loyal to him. They not only followed Gandhi, but also helped him in his experiments with life and India's struggle for freedom.

Harilal Gandhi

Kasturba Gandhi

Ramdas Gandhi

Kasturba with her four children in South Africa, 1902

Trusted aide

For 25 years, Mahadev Desai (1892–1942), a lawyer and writer, served Gandhi as his secretary. He was always by Gandhi's side as his friend and confidante. He also translated Gandhi's autobiography, *The Story of My Experiments with Truth*, into English.

"Truly my better half"

When Kastur Kapadia (1869–1944) married Gandhi, little did she know that she would come to be respected as *ba*, or "mother," in her country. She led an active life, traveling widely, addressing public meetings, running ashrams, and being at the forefront of many protests.

Bapu's children

Gandhi had a complicated relationship with his sons—Harilal, Manilal, Ramdas, and Devdas. Deprived of Gandhis attention and care, they bore the brunt of his offbeat ideas. They did not attend school or have a comfortable upbringing. The eldest son, Harilal, renounced his family. The other sons, however, joined Gandhi in India's freedom struggle.

Devdas Gandhi

Manilal Gandhi

Friend of the oppressed
Charles Freer Andrews (1871–1940), a British priest of the Church of England, came to India to teach philosophy. A great humanitarian and admirer of Gandhi's concept of nonviolence, Andrews is respected in India as Deenabandhu, or "friend of the oppressed."

Mirabehn at a spinning wheel, 1940

Finding a "treasure"
When Madeline Slade (1892–1982) joined Gandhi's Sabarmati Ashram in 1925, he said he had found "a treasure" and a daughter. Renamed Mirabehn, the Englishwoman became Gandhi's close ally, wore only *khadi*, and worked for India's freedom.

A leader emerges

When the British introduced the Rowlatt Act in 1919, curbing the freedom of the Indian people, Gandhi launched *satyagraha*, his nonviolent method of protest, for the first time in India. In response to his call, Indians came out in huge numbers. The protest was a great success, and it catapulted Gandhi onto the national stage. The unfair act and the Jallianwala Bagh massacre of innocent Indians, however, made Gandhi lose his faith in the British. He now began to aim for Indian self-rule.

Rowlatt Act

Named for Sidney Rowlatt, the judge who drafted the provisions, the Rowlatt Act came into force to stop anti-British activities. People could now be arrested simply on suspicion and kept in prison without trial for up to two years. Freedom of the press was also curtailed, as newspapers came under government control.

> *"(Rowlatt Commission recommendations) are unjust, subversive of the principles of liberty and justice... If the proposed measures are passed into law, we ought to offer* satyagraha.*"*
>
> MAHATMA GANDHI
> On the Rowlatt Report, 1919

Gandhi and Kasturba arrive at a mass rally, 1931

Nation on strike

The protest against the Rowlatt Act took the form of a dramatic one-day nationwide *hartal*, or strike. Indians in every part of the country skipped work that day to participate in the strike. Life ground to a halt, as stores shut down and schools were closed in response to Gandhi's call.

Jallianwala Bagh massacre

On April 13, 1919, a mass meeting took place in Jallianwala Bagh grounds in Amritsar, a town in northern India, against the Rowlatt Act. Brigadier-General REH Dyer ordered his soldiers to shoot at the unarmed crowd, which included women and children. Unable to escape from the enclosed park, more than 400 people were killed and 1,000 injured.

Tagore protests

Outraged by the Jallianwala Bagh tragedy, Rabindranath Tagore, poet and Nobel laureate, gave up the knighthood he had received from the British government. A commission was set up to look into the tragedy, but Brigadier-General Dyer was found not guilty.

News report carrying Tagore's letter to Lord Chelmsford, then Viceroy of India

Gandhi takes center stage

After the anti-Rowlatt *hartal*, Gandhi's stature grew. He was already a member of the Congress, the political party committed to fighting the foreign rule, but he now became its leader. In 1920, he wrote its new constitution, transforming it from a party of the elite to an organization of the common people.

Khilafat Movement

For all Muslims, the Ottoman Sultan was the *Khalifa*, or Caliph—their religious head. After the Ottoman Empire's defeat in World War I in 1919, Muslims feared that the Caliph would lose control over Islamic shrines. The Khilafat Movement was organized in India to voice Muslim outrage against the Britain's anti-Turkey policy. For Gandhi, this was a chance to forge a bond between Hindus and Muslims in India.

Ottoman Empire's coat of arms

Ottoman Empire
Ruled by a single family dynasty for seven centuries, the Ottoman (Turkish) Empire (1301–1922) stretched from Turkey to Egypt, eastern Europe, and West Asia. The Sultan was also the Caliph and controlled all Islamic shrines. When Turkey become a republic in 1924, the Caliph's position was abolished.

Procession of Khilafat supporters with a giant spinning wheel, Delhi, 1922

in the Devanagari script   God, in the Arabic script

Hindu-Muslim unity

For centuries, Hindus and Muslims had coexisted in India, developing a common culture, even sharing a dialect, Hindustani—a mix of Arabic, Persian, and Sanskrit—still spoken in some parts of India. Friction between the two communities, however, suited the British, who did not want them to unite. At Gandhi's behest, Hindus and Muslims formed a common front during the Khilafat Movement and displayed the strength of a united India.

Movement begins

The Khilafat Movement gathered steam when the Ottoman Empire was partitioned under the Treaty of Sèvres in 1920, and most Islamic shrines came under British control. Muslim leaders urged people to boycott British goods and institutions. With the end of the Caliphate in 1924, however, the movement lost its main purpose and soon fizzled out.

Khilafat and Gandhi

"... I would be an unworthy son of India if I did not stand by them (Muslims) in their hour of trial," said Gandhi. In 1920, the Congress, the main Indian political party, and the Khilafat leaders agreed to fight together for the causes of Khilafat and *swaraj* (self-rule).

Muhammad Ali Jinnah

A powerful Muslim leader, Muhammad Ali Jinnah opposed the Khilafat Movement, calling it an example of religious fanaticism. Jinnah until then was a member of the Congress and a votary of Hindu-Muslim unity. Later, he led the All-India Muslim League, a political party for Muslims, and demanded a separate state for Muslims.

Noncooperation
(1920-22)

Disappointed by the Rowlatt Act and Jallianwala incident, Gandhi launched the Noncooperation Movement against British rule. He traveled across India to explain his nonviolent campaign. People responded in droves, turning the movement into a mass uprising The British Raj was emphatically shaken for the first time and the goal of *swaraj*, or "self-rule," seemed within reach.

Nonviolent boycott

The Indian National Congress and the Khilafat leaders adopted Gandhi's program of "nonviolent noncooperation." People gave up their government jobs, students quit government-run schools and colleges, politicians avoided Raj councils, and volunteers courted arrest. Posters were printed that exhorted people to buy goods made in India.

A people stirred

Indians from all sections of society joined the campaign against the British. Students went to villages to preach *swadeshi*, urging people to use Indian goods. The Congress held public bonfires to burn foreign cloth. For the first time, women came out on the streets to protest, and nearly 30,000 people were arrested.

The Hindu symbol of swastika, believed to bring good luck

Chauri Chaura violence

On February 5, 1922, people participating in the Noncooperation Movement at Chauri Chaura, a town in northern India, turned violent. Angered when police fired shots, the crowd killed 22 policemen. Shaken by the violence and assuming responsibility for it, Gandhi called off the movement on February 11, 1922. On March 10, 1922, he was sentenced to six years in prison.

"Noncooperation with evil is as much a duty as is cooperation with good."

MAHATMA GANDHI
In a comment on the Noncooperation Movement, March 1922

Women confronting the police in Bombay (now Mumbai), 1930

Reawakening

When Gandhi called off the Noncooperation Movement in 1922, his colleagues and fellow Indians felt a deep sense of disappointment. For the next six years, the freedom struggle stalled. To fill the void and motivate people, Gandhi toured India, recommending constructive work such as spinning, fighting untouchability, and strengthening community ties.

Gandhi's autobiography in two volumes

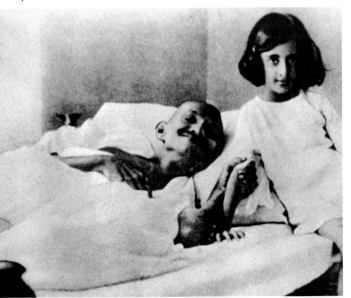

Gandhi with young Indira Gandhi, 1924

Prisoner, scholar, spinner

Convicted for inciting hatred against the British rule, Gandhi was imprisoned in 1922 at Yeravda jail in Poona (now Pune) in Maharashtra. Here, he read some 150 books, including Goethe's *Faust*. He also prayed and spun cloth regularly. After two years, he was released in 1924 to recover from surgery.

Fast for 21 days

Gandhi was released from prison only to face an India where Hindu-Muslim unity of the Khilafat years was a distant memory. When Hindus and Muslims attacked one another in September 1924 in Kohat, a town in northwest India, Gandhi fasted for 21 days in Muslim leader Muhammad Ali's home. Among his many visitors was a young Indira Gandhi, the future Prime Minister of India.

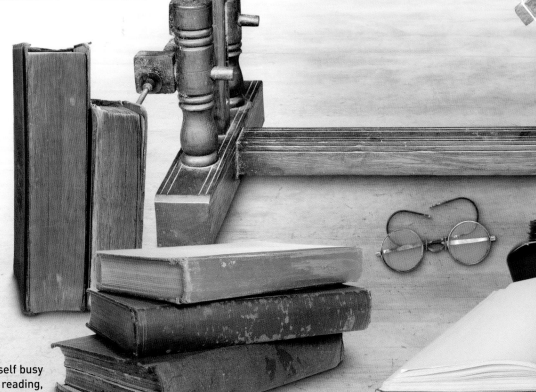

Gandhi kept himself busy in prison by reading, writing, and spinning

Protest denouncing the Simon Commission, Madras (now Chennai), in southern India, 1929

Charkha, *or the "spinning wheel"*

Gandhi and Nehru in Bombay (now Mumbai), 1942

Simon, go back

In February 1927, a Commission headed by Sir John Simon was sent by the British to India to recommend how the country could be governed in the future. No Indian was included in the panel, forcing an angry Congress party to boycott it. Indians protested in large numbers, shouting the slogan "Simon, go back." They were brutally beaten by the police.

Father figure

Gandhi worked tirelessly to unite different factions of the Congress. While senior leaders preferred a dominion status for India, remaining partly under British rule, younger leaders such as Jawaharlal Nehru pressed for full independence. In 1929, Gandhi succeeded in getting Nehru accepted as the Congress president.

Flag of freedom

On December 31, 1929, Jawaharlal Nehru unveiled the new Congress flag—with a *charkha* at its center—in Lahore (now in Pakistan). This was a formal declaration that the party was committed to *poorna swaraj*, or complete independence. Gandhi fixed January 26, 1930, as the date when all Indians would pledge themselves to freedom.

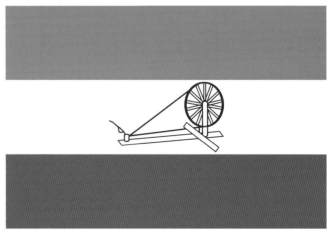

Untouchability

The caste system in India was based on a hierarchical way of organizing society. It continues today, although it is losing its stronghold on society. Under this system, society was divided into four groups, called varnas. Brahmins, the priestly class, formed the highest group; Kshatriyas were warriors; Vaishyas were traders; and the lowest class, the Shudras, provided manual labor. People who did the most menial tasks were considered outcastes, or untouchables.

Gandhi sweeping the floor in a 1964 sketch by cartoonist R. K. Laxman.

Leading by example

Gandhi was determined to eradicate the inhuman practice of untouchability. Although he belonged to the upper strata of society, he cleaned his own toilet—a job that only "untouchable" scavengers were supposed to do. Despite stiff opposition, he admitted an untouchable couple into his ashram. He also lived in homes of the untouchables whenever possible.

Cast out of society

In India, people who performed jobs considered unclean, such as scrubbing toilets or collecting garbage, were considered dirty. They were "untouchable", for it was believed their very touch would "pollute" others. They could not apply for better work or use the same temples or wells as those from higher castes.

An "untouchable" woman drawing water from a well outside her village

...made them 'mere recipients of charity."

Vaikom satyagraha

A famous temple for the Hindu god Mahadeva stands in Vaikom, Kerala, in southern India. The "untouchables" were not allowed to enter it or even walk on the roads around it. A *satyagraha*, supported by Gandhi, was launched in 1924 against this injustice. The "untouchables" tried to enter these roads peaceably, although they risked arrest and were subject to police brutality. Eventually, three roads were opened to them.

Ambedkar's stance

In the 1920s, Bhimrao Ramji Ambedkar, from the untouchable community, emerged as their leader. He fought for untouchables' right to elect their own representative in Parliament. In 1931, the British reserved some seats in Parliament for untouchables, but Gandhi feared this arrangement would widen the caste divide and he went on a fast in protest, forcing Ambedkar to withdraw his demand.

Untouchables today

The Constitution of India abolished untouchability in 1950. To improve the condition of this class of people, a portion of government jobs and places in higher education have been reserved for untouchables, now called Scheduled Castes or Dalits. Despite these measures, they continue to face social segregation and violence, especially in rural areas.

Gandhi and his peers

Although Gandhi was the unquestioned political leader and moral authority in the Congress party and the freedom movement, his contemporaries did not hesitate to express their differences on questions of goals and strategy. When Gandhi withdrew the Noncooperation Movement in 1922, or when he wanted to support the British during World War II, most Congress leaders disagreed with him. He found himself islolated when he proposed Jinnah's name for the prime ministership of free India.

Nightingale of India
Popularly called the "Nightingale of India," Sarojini Naidu (1879–1949) was a poet and a freedom fighter. In 1925, she became the first woman president of the Congress party. She played an active role in the Dandi March and Quit India Movement.

The chosen one
Jawaharlal Nehru (1889–1964) returned to India from Cambridge, England, in 1912 and joined the Congress party as a young representative. A protégé of Gandhi, whom he affectionately called *Bapu* (father), Nehru soon emerged as a leading proponent of full independence. Nehru went on to become the first Prime Minister of free India.

Champion of Muslims

Trained as a lawyer, Muhammad Ali Jinnah (1876–1948) began his political career with the Congress party. He left the party in 1920, unhappy with Gandhi's *satyagraha* methods. He became the Muslim League's permanent president, and, in 1940, demanded a separate state for Indian Muslims.

Pakistani one-rupee coin depicting Muhammad Ali Jinnah

Dissenting voice

Congress president in 1938 and 1939, Subhas Chandra Bose (1897–1945) left the party in 1939. A committed patriot, Bose differed from Gandhi, believing that Indians should wage an armed struggle against the British. During World War II, he allied with the Japanese to fight for India's freedom.

Iron Man of India

Vallabhbhai Patel (1875–1950) gave up his legal practice to join the freedom struggle. As a foremost Congress leader, he led peasant struggles against heavy taxes in Gujarat, forcing the British to revoke them. Patel became free India's first Home Minister. Often referred to as the "Iron Man of India," he worked hard to keep India united.

"Frontier Gandhi"

Khan Abdul Ghaffar Khan (1890–1988) was a political leader of the Pashtun people in the erstwhile North-West Frontier Province (now in Pakistan). A freedom fighter and a social reformer, he was so committed to nonviolence that he was called the "Frontier Gandhi." His organization—the *Khudai Khidmatgar* (Servants of God)—fought for India's freedom.

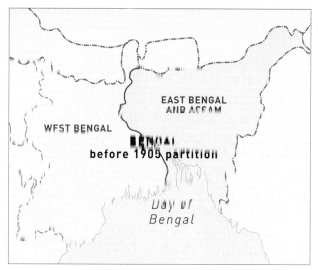

before 1905 partition

Roads to freedom

While the Mahatma's nonviolent method of struggle fired the imaginations of many Indians, there were those who believed in other approaches to attaining India's freedom. Even before Gandhi arrived on the political scene, the Congress party disagreed over which path to follow. Old-timers preferred to petition the British politely, while some younger members favored active protest. From 1905, bombings and assassinations also found some takers.

Birth of militancy
In 1905, Viceroy Lord Curzon enforced a partition of the Bengal province, saying it was too big. This was seen as a hateful British attempt to "divide and rule" India since Bengal was a center of Indian nationalism. Bengali anger gave birth to India's first militant freedom fighters, such as Aurobindo Ghose, and popularized protest methods, such as bonfires of British goods.

Moderates and extremists
The Indian National Congress was founded in 1885 to promote the participation of educated Indians in India's governance. In 1907, the party split into two factions—the moderates, who petitioned the British, and the extremists, who demanded self-rule. Extremist leader Bal Gangadhar Tilak was one of the first to say, "*Swaraj* is my birthright, and I shall have it!"

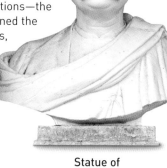

Statue of
Bal Gangadhar Tilak

Communist symbols hammer and sickle represent the working class

Communists
Formed in 1920 under the leadership of M. N. Roy, the Communist Party of India saw itself as the voice of poor Indian workers. It was often in opposition to the Congress, which it considered a party of elites. The communists supported the British in World War II, which made them unpopular with nationalist Indians.

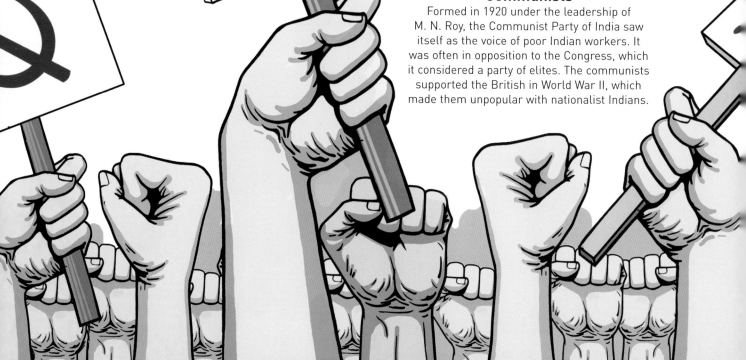

...hunger strike to demand fair treatment for Indian prisoners. He was hanged in 1931 at the age of 23.

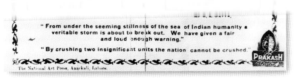

"From under the seeming stillness of the sea of Indian humanity a veritable storm is about to break out. We have given a fair and loud enough warning."

"By crushing two insignificant units the nation cannot be crushed."

Poster supporting Bhagat Singh and Batukeshwar Dutt's hunger strike

Chittagong uprising

On April 18, 1930, a group of revolutionaries, led by Surya Sen, a teacher, took over Chittagong (a town now in Bangladesh) for a day. They invaded British armories, cut communication lines between Calcutta and Chittagong, and declared a temporary government. Sen and others were hanged in 1934.

Statue of Surya Sen

Indian National Army

Impatient with Gandhi's nonviolent methods, Congress leader Subhas Chandra Bose left India in 1939. During World War II, he joined the Axis Powers to fight the British. He even met Adolf Hitler for support. He formed the Indian National Army (INA) with Indians living in Malaya, Singapore, and Burma and fought the British in northeast India.

Sleeve patch for a regiment of INA in Germany

Gandhi's letter appealing for support for the Dandi March

Raised clenched fists, signifying strength and unity

"Pen is mightier than the sword"

As much as he admired the courage of revolutionaries such as Bhagat Singh, Gandhi believed that violence caused only harm. He always negotiated with his opponents before launching a political struggle. He wrote thousands of letters and articles to garner support for the Indian cause.

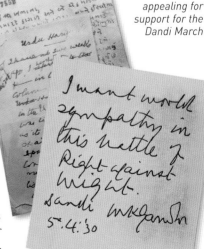

43

March to the sea

On January 26, 1930, declaring full independence as their goal, Indians pledged with Gandhi that "it was a crime against man and God to submit to British rule." Confident that people were ready for a new push for independence, Gandhi launched another civil disobedience movement in March 1930. Aware that Indians resented the British government's monopoly to make salt, Gandhi based his new movement on this vital ingredient of the Indian diet. The resistance spread like wildfire, attracting volunteers from across the country.

All about salt

Gandhi had good reasons for disobeying the salt law, which not only prohibited the manufacture and sale of salt by Indians but also deprived the poor of their livelihood. Gandhi was also aware of the symbolic appeal of salt to people of all religions, castes, and classes. Making and selling it, in breach of the law, was a simple and effective act of protest open to all Indians.

Breaking the salt law

On March 12, 1930, Gandhi embarked on a historic march to Dandi, a village on Gujarat's coast. Gandhi and his followers left the Sabarmati Ashram to walk 220 miles (354km) to Dandi. Thousands of people joined them along the way. On April 6 Gandhi lifted a fistful of salt and broke the law. Despite his arrest, the movement continued

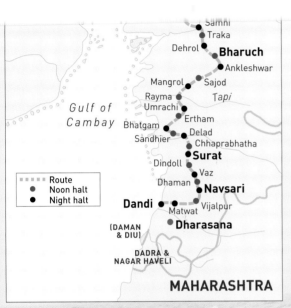

Samni
Traka
Dehrol **Bharuch**
Ankleshwar
Mangrol Sajod
Rayma *Tapi*
Umrachi
Gulf of Cambay Ertham
Bhatgam Delad
Sandhier Chhaprabhatha
Dindoll **Surat**
Vaz
Dhaman
Navsari
Dandi
Matwat Vijalpur
(DAMAN & DIU) **Dharasana**
DADRA & NAGAR HAVELI
MAHARASHTRA

Route
Noon halt
Night halt

Route map of the Dandi March in Gujarat (also showing Dharasana)

Government responds

Indian protesters not only openly made salt but also went on mass strikes and picketed foreign goods. The authorities responded to this civil disobedience with ruthlessness. They outlawed the Congress Working Committee, imprisoned more than 90,000 people—including Gandhi—and unleashed force on protesters.

Dharasana satyagraha

From Dandi, the movement spread to other parts of India. In May 1930, Gandhi declared a raid on the salt depots at Dharasana, 25 miles (40km) from Dandi. The volunteers marched peacefully but were brutally beaten by police. Thousands were sent to jail.

Lord Irwin, Viceroy of India from 1926 to 1931

In the eyes of the world

The incredible courage of the marchers at Dharasana shook the conscience of the world. Reports appeared in many international newspapers and journals, such as *Münchner Illustrierte Presse*, a German magazine. Journalist Webb Miller's eyewitness report described how the police rained blows... with "steel-shod *lathis*" while "not one marcher even raised an arm...."

Gandhi-Irwin Pact

In February 1931, after his release from prison, Gandhi signed a pact with Viceroy Lord Irwin that freed the salt march prisoners, allowed peaceful picketing of foreign goods, removed the ban on the Congress party, and permitted people in coastal areas to make their own salt.

Trip to England

As the only representative of the Indian National Congress at the Second Round Table Conference, Gandhi sailed for London in August 1931. Held by the British to discuss India's future with Indian leaders, the Conference proved to be a failure for Gandhi. His claim that the Congress represented all Indians was rejected by the other Indian delegates, and the British did not agree to his demand for self-rule. Nonetheless, he spent two months in England meeting people.

Gandhi disembarks from the ocean liner *SS Rajputana* at Marseille, France, enroute to England

Round Table Conference

Indian delegates at the Second Round Table Conference in September 1931 included princes, religious leaders, and B. R. Ambedkar, who represented the "untouchables"—the lowest caste in India's social hierarchy. At the meeting, many leaders demanded elections in which each community voted for its representatives separately. Gandhi, however, was of the opinion that such a measure would further divide the people of India.

"... no matter what the fortunes may be of this Round Table Conference, I consider that it was well worth my paying this visit to England..."

MAHATMA GANDHI
Speech at Kingsley Hall,
East London, October 17, 1931

Gandhi being cheered by women from the cotton mills, Lancashire, England, 1931

Meeting Charlie Chaplin

In London, Gandhi met comedian Charlie Chaplin, the silent-movie star. Gandhi agreed to meet him when he was told that Chaplin honored the poor in his films. Hundreds of people thronged to see the two famous men in Canning Town in east London.

Two sides of a
1931 British coin

Portrait of
King George V

Europe calling

While in Europe, Gandhi spent time in Switzerland and Italy with his friend and biographer, Romain Rolland, who wrote of how "a hurricane" of people gathered to meet the "king of India."

St. Peter's
Basilica,
Rome, Italy

Mahatma and the Monarch

While in London, Gandhi was invited to an imperial reception by King George V and Queen Mary. Despite the protocol for formal attire, Gandhi attended the reception in his usual *dhoti*, or loincloth, which he wore to associate himself with poor Indians. When asked if he felt uncomfortable, he quipped, "The king has enough on for both of us."

World War II and India

World War II (1939–45) involved more than 30 nations and over 100 million combatants. Germany, along with Italy and Japan, formed the Axis Powers, which fought Britain, the US, the Soviet Union, and France—the main Allied Powers. As a British colony, India sent more than two million soldiers to the war.

Gandhi and Hitler

The causes of WWII are complex. One factor was the ambition of Adolf Hitler, the dictator of Germany, who believed that Germans were a superior race meant to rule the world. Hitler's Nazi Party sent Germany's Jews to concentration camps, where six million died. In 1939, Gandhi wrote to Hitler, asking him to "... prevent a war which may reduce humanity to the savage state."

Congress and the war

Many Congress party members wanted to offer support to the British in the war effort, but only in return for a promise of Indian independence. Britain, however, involved India in the war without even consulting India's leaders. Gandhi eventually gave a call to the British to "Quit India." In return, the British propaganda machine accused Gandhi of supporting the Axis Powers.

World War II poster showing an Indian in the British army

Gandhi wrote to both US president
Franklin D. Roosevelt and China's leader
Chiang Kai Shek, saying that the Allied
Powers could station troops in India to check
Japanese aggression. He pointed out though
that the Allies' claim of fighting for freedom
was hollow if Britain continued to rule India.

Chiang Kai Shek with Franklin D. Roosevelt

INA war medal

A British officer
leading Indian
soldiers in
Egypt, 1940

ndian troops in WWII

illions of Indian soldiers fought for the British
the war, in places as far-flung as northern Africa
nd the Middle East. They also fought the Japanese in
urma (now Myanmar) and near India's northeastern
egion and played a key role in liberating Singapore and
ong Kong from the Japanese, who surrendered in 1945.

Quit India Movement

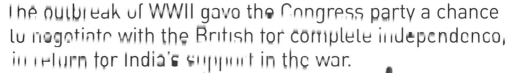

The outbreak of WWII gave the Congress party a chance to negotiate with the British for complete independence, in return for India's support in the war. The British, however, involved India in WWII without consulting the Congress. By the time the Cripps Mission came to India to negotiate the provisions for self-rule, Gandhi had already decided to launch another mass movement.

Indian national flag

Cripps Mission

By January 1942, WWII had reached India's doorstep, and the British were forced to seek Indian help. Sir Stafford Cripps, a member of Winston Churchill's War Cabinet—came to India with the offer of a government that would include Indians on the Viceroy's Executive Council. Talks broke down when the Congress demanded that an Indian be defense member of the Council.

"Quit India"

On July 14, 1942, Gandhi and other leaders met at Wardha, in western India, and passed a resolution demanding total freedom from British rule. While members of the Congress supported Gandhi, the Muslim League opposed his move. The top leaders of the Congress party met again in Bombay (now Mumbai) on August 8 and voted unanimously in favor of the resolution.

Movement begins

On August 8, Gandhi made a stirring speech in Bombay, exhorting people to "do or die" and urging them to "act as if you are free." Nationwide strikes and demonstrations followed. Some areas, such as Satara, in western India, established parallel governments, declaring themselves free.

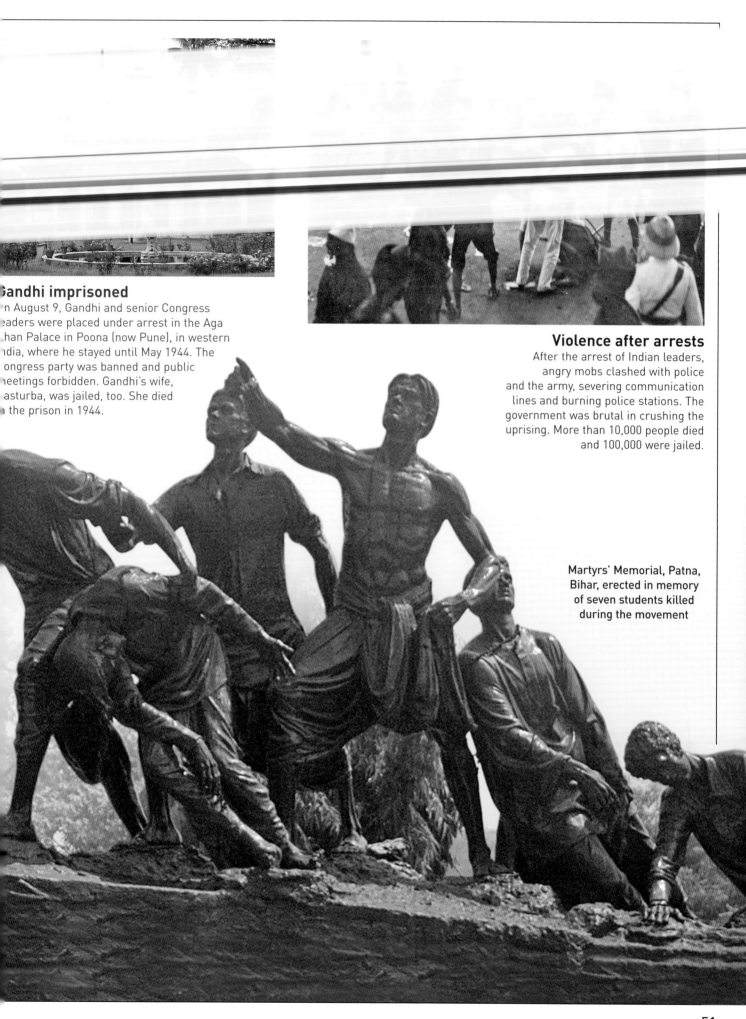

Gandhi imprisoned

On August 9, Gandhi and senior Congress leaders were placed under arrest in the Aga Khan Palace in Poona (now Pune), in western India, where he stayed until May 1944. The Congress party was banned and public meetings forbidden. Gandhi's wife, Kasturba, was jailed, too. She died in the prison in 1944.

Violence after arrests

After the arrest of Indian leaders, angry mobs clashed with police and the army, severing communication lines and burning police stations. The government was brutal in crushing the uprising. More than 10,000 people died and 100,000 were jailed.

Martyrs' Memorial, Patna, Bihar, erected in memory of seven students killed during the movement

Search for harmony

Gandhi's vision of India was one of a country united. He spared no effort in trying to bring Hindus and Muslims together. In the 1920s, the two religious communities joined forces to fight the colonial government, with considerable success. For their part, the British did their best to inflame the differences between the two religions

Shared culture

Hindus and Muslims had lived peacefully in the subcontinent for centuries. The two religions were part of one civilization, sharing elements of food, clothing, architecture, and art. Indian architecture, for instance, often shows a blend of Hindu and Muslim styles. In Ganesh Pol, the arched gateway in Amber Fort, Rajasthan, floral patterns in the Islamic style flank an image of the Hindu god Ganesh.

Divide and rule

The British policy of "divide and rule" encouraged divisions between Indian communities. In 1909, John Morley, secretary of state of India, introduced a system of "separate electorates," in which Muslims were able to elect their representatives in government councils separate from Hindus. This deepened the religious divide that already existed between Hindus and Muslims.

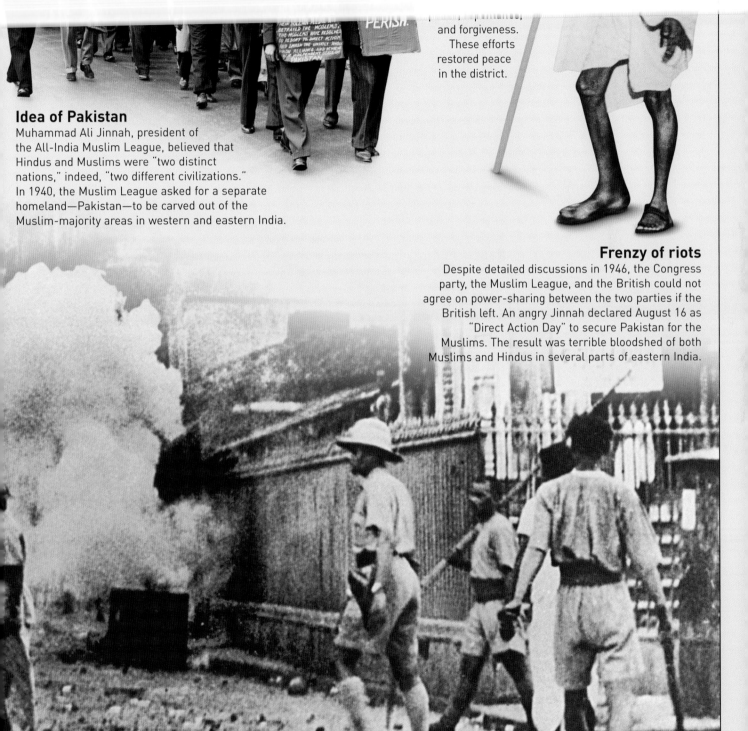

Idea of Pakistan

Muhammad Ali Jinnah, president of
the All-India Muslim League, believed that
Hindus and Muslims were "two distinct
nations," indeed, "two different civilizations."
In 1940, the Muslim League asked for a separate
homeland—Pakistan—to be carved out of the
Muslim-majority areas in western and eastern India.

and forgiveness.
These efforts
restored peace
in the district.

Frenzy of riots

Despite detailed discussions in 1946, the Congress
party, the Muslim League, and the British could not
agree on power-sharing between the two parties if the
British left. An angry Jinnah declared August 16 as
"Direct Action Day" to secure Pakistan for the
Muslims. The result was terrible bloodshed of both
Muslims and Hindus in several parts of eastern India.

Cabinet Mission

In March 1946, Britain sent three cabinet ministers to hold discussions with the Indian leaders about how power should be transferred. Congress party leaders and Muhammad Ali Jinnah could not agree on how the Muslim-majority areas of India would be ruled. A partition of the country seemed inevitable.

Partition

From 1940 onward, Muhammad Ali Jinnah and the Muslim League lobbied for a separate nation for Indian Muslims. For Gandhi, separation was unacceptable. Other Congress leaders, however, became resigned to partition because of the rising discord between Hindus and Muslims. Independence thus came hand in hand with partition. Millions were uprooted, amid riots and killings.

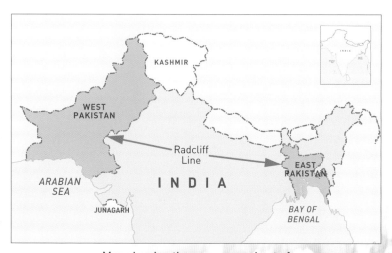

Map showing the areas carved out of undivided India to create East and West Pakistan

Radcliff Line

Sir Cyril Radcliff, a British lawyer, was tasked with setting the border between India and Pakistan. His job was to divide 175,000 square miles (4,53,200 square km) of land, rivers, roads, and about 88 million people. Radcliff, who had never been to India, was given just five weeks to complete the work. He was also in a hurry to leave because the climate did not suit him.

Mass exodus

Hindus and Sikhs from the newly created Pakistan migrated to India, and Indian Muslims to Pakistan, leaving behind their ancestral homes. More than 14 million people moved—on foot, in carts, and in inhumanly packed trains, with people spilling onto the roofs. Horrific killings took place on both sides of the border.

Indian troops landing in Srinagar, Kashmir, 1947

ne-man force

s India was partitioned, a saddened
andhi chose to fast and hold common
ayer meetings for Hindus and Muslims in
alcutta (now Kolkata), in eastern India. Lord
ountbatten, the last British Viceroy of India,
id, "In Punjab we have 55,000 soldiers and
rge-scale rioting... in Bengal our forces
nsist of one man, and there is no riot."

Freedom at last!

After decades of struggle, India's independence was at hand. Exhausted by World War II, the British could not hold on to India any longer. In 1947, the British announced India's independence and also its partition into two countries—India and Pakistan. Violent Hindu-Muslim riots followed, the bloodshed saddened the Mahatma and marred the joy of freedom.

Mountbatten Plan

Admiral Louis Mountbatten, the last British Viceroy of India, was in charge of overseeing India's independence. On June 3, 1947, he announced that if the legislative assemblies of Punjab and Bengal, where a majority of Muslims lived, voted for partition, the two provinces would be divided between India and Pakistan.

Pakistan is born

Under the partition agreement, Muslim-majority areas in the northwest and northeast of British India formed the state of Pakistan. The new country came into existence on August 14, 1947—a date that is sacred in the Islamic calendar. Muhammed Ali Jinnah was sworn in as the first Governor-General of Pakistan. He also came to be known as *Quaid-e-Azam*, or the "Great Leader," of the newly created country.

Father of the Nation

On Independence Day, as India rejoiced, Mahatma Gandhi—the "Father of the Nation"—chose to remain in an abandoned Muslim house in Calcutta (now Kolkata), in the eastern part of India. He mourned the partition of the country and the terrible riots by observing August 15 as a day of fasting and prayer.

"At the stroke of the midnight hour, when the world sleeps, India will awake to life and freedom."

PANDIT JAWAHARLAL NEHRU
On the eve of India's Independence, August 14, 1947

Border Security Force personnel at a flag-hoisting ceremony in Attari, Punjab

Independence Day celebrations

Every year, on August 15, India celebrates Independence Day. The prime minister hoists the national flag and gives a speech to the nation at the Red Fort in the Indian capital, New Delhi. Flag-raising ceremonies take place all over the country on this day. Indians also pay their respects to the freedom fighters who made it possible for them to live in a free country.

January 1948
In the final month of his life, Gandhi found himself in a partitioned India where people were full of fear and hatred. Delhi, the capital, received millions of Hindu and Sikh refugees from Pakistan. The Muslims of Delhi, feeling unsafe, wanted to leave. On January 13, Gandhi went on his last fast, asking for a "reunion of hearts."

Godse, who fired three fatal shots at Gandhi. A Hindu nationalist, Godse blamed Gandhi for sacrificing Hindu interests and appeasing Muslims. Godse and coconspirator, Narayan Apte, were hanged in 1949.

"Hey Ram!"

MAHATMA GANDHI
Uttering Lord Rama's name, seconds before his death, January 30, 1948

Ashes to ashes

The news of Gandhi's death came from Prime Minister Nehru, who said on the radio, "The light has gone out of our lives...." More than two million grief-stricken mourners joined Gandhi's funeral procession from Birla House to the Yamuna River in Delhi. Following Hindu tradition, Gandhi was cremated and his ashes scattered in the Ganga River at Allahabad, a city in northern India.

World reacts

"India Shaken, World Mourns" read the headline in the *New York Times*, as tributes and condolences poured in from world luminaries—the Pope, Albert Einstein, US President Harry S. Truman, and England's King George, among countless others. They called Gandhi "a giant among men" whose death was a loss to humankind.

Gandhi's funeral procession, February 6, 1948

In Gandhi's footsteps

Even after his death, Gandhi continued to set an example for millions around the world, especially those struggling to change unfair and exploitive conditions in their own countries. Leaders such as Martin Luther King, Jr., Nelson Mandela, and Aung San Suu Kyi found motivation in Gandhi's beliefs and strategies of nonviolent transformation.

MANDELA RELEASED!

FREE ALL POLITICAL PRISONERS!

Martin Luther King, Jr.

A pastor and leader of the Civil Rights Movement in the US, Martin Luther King, Jr. (1929–68) strove to bring social and legal equality to African Americans, who were denied equal opportunities, their civil liberties, and often their voting rights. He acknowledged Gandhi's teachings to be his "guiding light."

Martin Luther King, Jr. leading a march in Alabama, 1965

Nelson Mandela

Inspired by Gandhi's methods of nonviolent resistance, Nelson Mandela (1918–2013) fought apartheid—the policy of racial discrimination against blacks—followed in South Africa since 1948. He was imprisoned for 27 years. He became South Africa's first black president in 1994.

Albert Einstein

Passionately opposed to war, Albert Einstein (1879–1955) was a great German-American physicist and Nobel laureate. He once wrote to Gandhi, "You have shown it is possible to succeed without violence...." On his 70th birthday, he said, "Generations to come... will scarce believe that such a man... walked upon this Earth."

John Lennon

British musician, founding member of the The Beatles, and the writer of stirring songs such as "Give Peace a Chance," John Lennon (1940–80) was an admirer of Gandhi and his principle of nonviolence. Lennon and his wife, Yoko Ono, were peace activists who campaigned against the Vietnam War.

Aung San Suu Kyi

Nobel Peace Prize winner Aung San Suu Kyi (b. 1945) has struggled for democracy and against military rule in her country, Myanmar, for much of her life. She has often cited Gandhi's life and work as her inspiration to fight the oppressive regime in her country.

Congressional medal awarded to Suu Kyi by the US, 2008

Barack Obama

"I might not be standing before you today, as president of the United States, had it not been for Gandhi..." The US's first African-American president, Barack Obama (b. 1961), often quotes Gandhi as his inspiration to spread the message that we personally "be" the change that we seek in the world, and that ordinary people can do extraordinary things.

Nonviolence in action

For Gandhi, being fearless and not giving in to hatred were two crucial pillars of nonviolence—a philosophy that continues to appeal to people across the world. The 20th century witnessed moments of intense political conflict in which ordinary people embarked on dramatic protests, yet remained peaceful. From leaders such as Václav Havel to Lech Wałęsa, these activists showed how nonviolence could transform the world.

Rosa Parks, United States

In the 1950s, almost all African Americans in the US attended segregated schools. On buses, blacks were expected to give up their seats to whites, if asked. On December 1, 1955, Rosa Parks (1913–2005), a seamstress and civil rights' activist in Montgomery, Alabama, refused to surrender her seat and was arrested. African Americans launched a city-wide boycott of buses, focing the city to lift the law requiring segregated buses.

Solidarity Movement, Poland

Frustrated by the lack of freedom in Communist Poland in the 1980s, people joined Solidarity— a trade union led by Lech Wałęsa (b. 1943). Enjoying the support of the Catholic Church, Solidarity organized mass strikes, without once turning violent. Wałęsa won the Nobel Peace Prize in 1983. When the government was forced to concede free elections in 1989, he became the president of Poland.

A 1990 coin issued to celebrate Solidarity's 10-year struggle

American flower power

In an anti-Vietnam War rally in 1967, thousands of students marched to the Pentagon in Washington, D.C., placing flowers in the guns of soldiers as a sign of peace. The war, fought between North Vietnam (supported by the Soviet Union and China) and South Vietnam (supported by the US), was viewed by many to be unjust, evoking widespread anger in the US.

Unknown protester blocks a military convoy at Tiananmen Square in Beijing, China, 1989

Tiananmen Square, China

Celebrating the date on which the Velvet Revolution began — 17.11.1989

Velvet Revolution, Czechoslovakia

Starting in 1948, Czechoslovakia (now the Czech Republic and Slovakia) was ruled by the Communist Party. In November 1989, students and workers took to the streets in an antigovernment march. The police reacted with force, beating the protesters, who remained peaceful. The nonviolent revolution resulted in the overthrow of the government. That same year, Václav Havel (1936–2011) was elected president of the new republic.

Lady in red, Turkey

In 2013, Turkey erupted in protest against the country's authoritarian government. Initially directed at the government's plan to destroy Gazi Park, a tiny green patch in Istanbul, the rallies soon turned into huge demonstrations. As the police used force against protesters, Ceyda Sungur, a peaceful demonstrator, was attacked with tear gas. Her picture became a symbol of the government's ruthlessness, aiding the cause.

Timeline

Gandhi's story is not an ordinary recounting of his life events. Whether it was his childhood years in Gujarat, the time he spent in South Africa, or the heady days of India's freedom struggle, these are phases in history that either shaped his world view or were influenced by his ideals.

October 2, 1869
Mohandas Karamchand Gandhi is born into a Modh Bania family in Gujarat.

Young Gandhi with his brother Laxmidas

1883
Mohandas marries Kastur Kapadia at the age of 13.

1869

18

1903
Gandhi founds *Indian Opinion*, a journal for Indians in South Africa.

1904
He founds Phoenix Settlement in South Africa, as an experiment in community living.

1906
Zulu Rebellion breaks out; Gandhi sets up an ambulance corps.

Zulu warrior

1907
Gandhi launches a protest against the anti-Indian Transvaal Registration Act.

1908
Gandhi leads 2,000 Indians in burning their registration certificates in Johannesburg.

1910
Gandhi sets up Tolstoy Farm in South Africa.

1912
He accompanies Indian leader Gopal Krishna Gokhale on a tour of South Africa.

1913
He leads a Great March of thousands of Indians to the Transvaal.

1902　1904　1906　1908　1910　1912

1925
Gandhi writes his autobiography, *The Story of My Experiments with Truth*.

Sea salt

1928
Residents of Gujarat successfully protest against high rents, using methods of noncooperation inspired by Gandhi.

1930
On January 26, Indians take Gandhi's pledge of *poorna swaraj*, the first formal declaration that the Congress party wanted complete independence.

1930
Dandi March begins against British monopoly of salt; Gandhi and several others are imprisoned.

1931
Gandhi attends the Second Round Table Conference in London.

1932
Gandhi sent to Yeravda Jail for sedition; fasts against separate electorates for Harijans.

1936
Gandhi founds Sevagram Ashram in Wardha to serve poor villagers and the "untouchables."

1933
He founds *Harijan* newspaper; gives the name "Harijan," or "Children of God," to "untouchables."

1926　1928　1930　1932　1934　1936

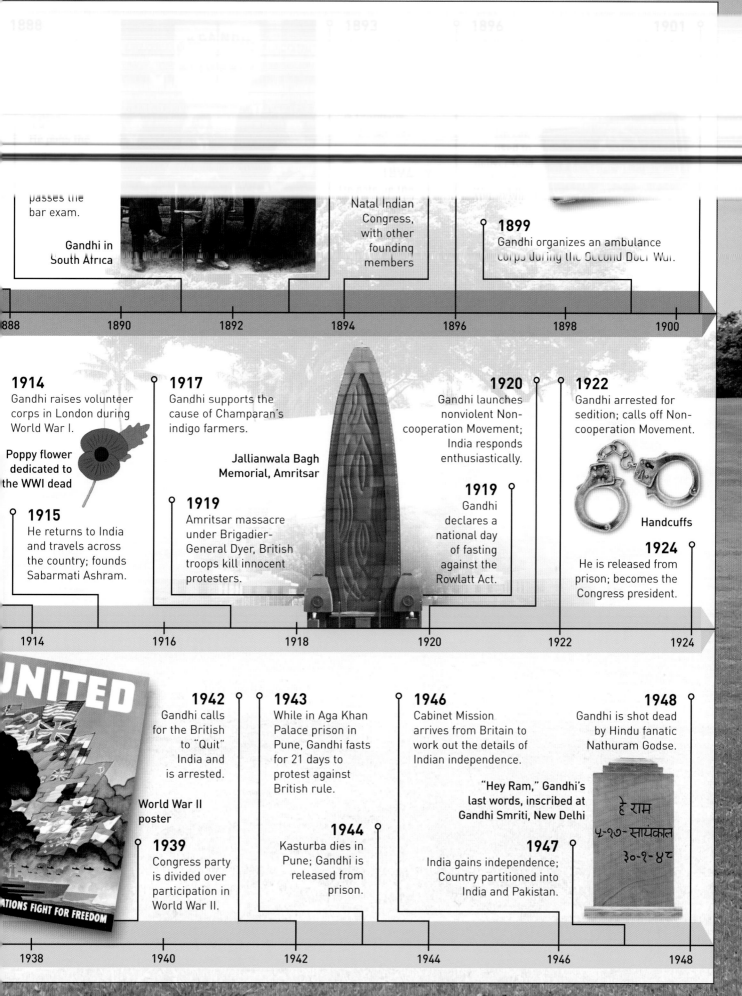

passes the bar exam.

Gandhi in South Africa

Natal Indian Congress, with other founding members

1899
Gandhi organizes an ambulance corps during the Second Boer War.

888   1890   1892   1894   1896   1898   1900

1914
Gandhi raises volunteer corps in London during World War I.

Poppy flower dedicated to the WWI dead

1915
He returns to India and travels across the country; founds Sabarmati Ashram.

1917
Gandhi supports the cause of Champaran's indigo farmers.

Jallianwala Bagh Memorial, Amritsar

1919
Amritsar massacre under Brigadier-General Dyer, British troops kill innocent protesters.

1920
Gandhi launches nonviolent Non-cooperation Movement; India responds enthusiastically.

1919
Gandhi declares a national day of fasting against the Rowlatt Act.

1922
Gandhi arrested for sedition; calls off Non-cooperation Movement.

Handcuffs

1924
He is released from prison; becomes the Congress president.

1914   1916   1918   1920   1922   1924

1942
Gandhi calls for the British to "Quit" India and is arrested.

World War II poster

1939
Congress party is divided over participation in World War II.

1943
While in Aga Khan Palace prison in Pune, Gandhi fasts for 21 days to protest against British rule.

1944
Kasturba dies in Pune; Gandhi is released from prison.

1946
Cabinet Mission arrives from Britain to work out the details of Indian independence.

"Hey Ram," Gandhi's last words, inscribed at Gandhi Smriti, New Delhi

1947
India gains independence; Country partitioned into India and Pakistan.

1948
Gandhi is shot dead by Hindu fanatic Nathuram Godse.

हे राम
५-१७-सायंकाल
३०-१-४८

NITED

TIONS FIGHT FOR FREEDOM

1938   1940   1942   1944   1946   1948

Did you know?

FASCINATING FACTS ABOUT GANDHI

Gandhi was such a prolific writer that the compilation of his letters and articles, *The Collected Works of Mahatma Gandhi*, has been published in 100 volumes.

Gandhi was ambidextrous—he could write with both hands. He could spin with both hands as well.

When Gandhi first bacame a lawyer, he was so terrified of public speaking that he panicked in the courtroom and was unable to represent his client.

Gandhi shares his birthday (October 2) with American comedian Groucho Marx and English writer Graham Greene. Marx and Gandhi wore the same kind of round eyeglasses, sported similar moustaches, and were known for their witty remarks.

Groucho Marx

India observes only three national holidays—Independence Day on August 15, Republic Day on January 26, and Gandhi's birthday on October 2. This birthday is also observed as the International Day of Nonviolence.

Five Nobel Peace Prize winners—Martin Luther King, Jr., Aung San Suu Kyi, Nelson Mandela, Adolfo Pérez Esquivel, and Barack Obama have acknowledged Gandhi's influence on their world view. Gandhi, however, never won a Nobel Prize.

World Peace gong at
Gandhi Smriti Museum, New Delhi

Exhibited in the Gandhi Smriti Museum, New Delhi, the World Peace gong commemorates the centenary of Gandhi's first *satyagraha* in South Africa in 1906. It depicts the flags of all member countries of the United Nations and symbols of world religions. It was presented by the Multi-Cultural Society of Indonesia in 2006.

Gandhi's footsteps, marking his final walk at Gandhi Smriti, New Delhi

Gandhi was the first "colored" lawyer to be admitted to the Supreme Court in South Africa. (Asians, who were neither white nor black, were called "colored" at this time in South Africa.)

Gandhi joined the Second Boer War in 1902 as a Sergeant-Major. He fought on the British side.

Gandhi first came across a *charkha*, or "spinning wheel," in 1915 at the age of 46.

When Gandhi's wife, Kasturba, died in prison, she was dressed in a saree made of yarn spun by Gandhi.

Gandhi owned fewer than 10 items, which included his watch, eyeglasses, and sandals. He stayed in ashrams most of his life and never owned a house.

Poster of the movie
Lage Raho Munna Bhai

Gandhi never visited the US. Among his many admirers in the country was industrialist Henry Ford, who sent him a letter praising his nonviolent campaign against British rule.

Gandhi was a committed follower of naturopathy. When sick, he never took medicine, preferring to cure himself by fasting, massages, and special diets.

always kept a picture of Gandhi with him. Apple's "Think Different" advertising campaign featured an image of Gandhi.

Gandhi was always punctual. Before his assassination on January 30, 1948, he was upset that he was 10 minutes late for the evening prayer.

Several movies about Gandhi have been made. Richard Attenborough's *Gandhi* (1982) won eight Academy Awards—the highest for any biographical movie based on real events. In India, Hindi films *Lage Raho Munna Bhai* (2006) and *Gandhi, My Father* (2007) are two famous films based on Gandhi's life.

Garlic

Natural remedies advocated by Gandhi

Onion

Castor oil plant

Crushed turmeric

Turmeric root

Gandhi found great peace in nursing the sick. As a boy, he tended to his ailing father. He devoted two hours a day in a charitable hospital in South Africa, gave therapeutic cures to residents of his ashrams in India, and even dressed the wounds of lepers.

Gandhi was once operated on in prison. A British nurse teased him, saying, "You... owed your life to the skill of a British surgeon... administering British drugs and to the ministrations of a British nurse!"

Gandhi was an extraordinary walker. As a law student in London, he often walked for miles a day to save money. During the Dandi March, he walked 9 miles (15km) every day. At the age of 77, he walked barefoot from village to village for two months on his peace mission in Noakhali, East Bengal (now a part of Bangladesh).

Gandhi's funeral procession in Delhi was 5-miles (8-km) long and was joined by more than two million grief-stricken people from Birla House to Yamuna River.

Every major city in India has a Mahatma Gandhi Road—as do Paris in France, Durban in South Africa, and Tehran in Iran.

More than 70 countries have erected statues of Gandhi and issued postage stamps honoring him.

US stamp bearing Gandhi's image, 1961

Mapping Gandhi

Mahatma Gandhi continues to be celebrated in many countries in many ways. On his birth centenary in 1969, more than 40 countries, including the UK, released postage stamps to honor Gandhi. Statues of him are found in cities in more than 70 countries. In India, it is hard to miss Gandhi—with his portrait on the currency and statues in every major city.

PLACES TO VISIT IN INDIA

- National Gandhi Museum and Library, New Delhi
- Kirti Mandir, Porbandar
- Sabarmati Ashram and Museum, Ahmedabad
- Mani Bhavan Gandhi Sangrahalaya, Mumbai
- Magan Sangrahalaya, Wardha
- National Gandhi Memorial Society, Pune
- Gandhi Sangrahalaya, Patna
- Gandhi Bhavan, Thycaud, Trivandrum
- Gandhi Memorial Museum, Madurai
- Gandhi Memorial Museum, Kolkata

Iceland

Canada

NORTH AMERICA

United States of America

ATLANTIC OCEAN

M

Mexico

Cuba

Mauri

The Gambia
Guinea-Bissa
Sierra Le
Lib

Nicaragua

Trinidad and Tobago

Panama

Venezuela

Guyana
French Guiana
Surinam

Peru

Brazil

PACIFIC OCEAN

Bolivia

SOUTH AMERICA

Chile

Uruguay

Argentina

Map of India (highlighted places associated with Gandhi)

JAMMU AND KASHMIR

PAKISTAN

HIMACHAL PRADESH

Amritsar
PUNJAB
Shimla
UTTARANCHAL

HARYANA

CHINA

New Delhi

Jaipur

Lucknow

NEPAL

SIKKIM

BHUTAN

ARUNACHAL PRADESH

ASSAM

Guwahati
NAGALAND
MEGHALAYA
MANIPUR

RAJASTHAN

UTTAR PRADESH

Patna
BIHAR

Khajuraho

JHARKHAND

BANGLADESH

TRIPURA

MIZORAM

GUJARAT

Ahmedabad
Baroda

MADHYA PRADESH

Ranchi

WEST BENGAL

Kolkata

MYANMAR

Porbandar

Wardha

CHHATTISGARH

ORISSA

Bhubaneswar

Mumbai

MAHARASHTRA

Pune

Hyderabad

Bay of Bengal

Arabian Sea

ANDHRA PRADESH

GOA

KARNATAKA

Andaman and Nicobar Islands

Bangalore

Chennai

Puducherry

Kavindapadi

KERALA

TAMIL NADU

Madurai

Trivandrum

SRI LANKA

INDIAN OCEAN

Map of India highlighting places associated with Gandhi

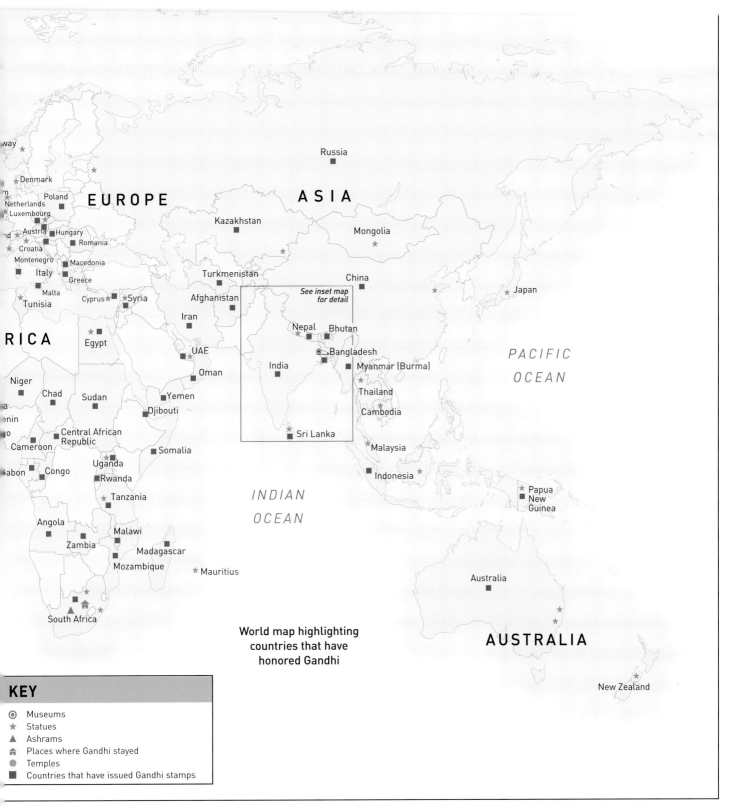

World map highlighting
countries that have
honored Gandhi

KEY

- ⊙ Museums
- ★ Statues
- ▲ Ashrams
- ⌂ Places where Gandhi stayed
- ● Temples
- ■ Countries that have issued Gandhi stamps

Glossary

Example of the type of portable *charkha* used by Gandhi

ALLIED POWERS Britain, France, and Russia—the countries allied against the Central Powers (Germany, Austria-Hungary, and the Ottoman Empire) in World War I. In World War II, Britain, France, the Soviet Union, and the US, among other countries, fought the Axis Powers, led by Germany, Italy, and Japan.

An illustration featuring the military allies and their flags during World War I

APARTHEID The official system of racial segregation practiced in South Africa between 1948 and 1994. Under the system, blacks and "coloreds" did not get the same political rights as whites.

ASHRAM A spiritual retreat, usually away from an urban center, where people dedicate themselves to religious activities and meditation.

ASSASSINATION Murder of a public figure for political, social, or religious reasons.

AXIS POWERS The countries that supported Germany during World War II, chiefly Italy and Japan.

BANIA In Indian society a person belonging to a caste traditionally involved in trading, moneylending, or shopkeeping.

BRAHMIN One of the four broad social groups, or *varna*—Brahmin, Kshatriya, Vaishya, and Shudra—that make up the traditional Indian caste system. The Brahmins—the highest in the hierarchical caste structure—are priests, scholars, or teachers.

CASTE SYSTEM The traditional Indian system of grouping people as "higher" or "lower" in the social order as per the nature of their work. People were born into their father's caste, did the same work, and married only within their caste.

CHARKHA Hindi for "spinning wheel."

CIVIL DISOBEDIENCE A nonviolent form of protest in which the protesters refuse to obey laws that they consider unjust.

COLONY A territory ruled by a foreign country. Also a territory inhabited by a large number of foreigners who go on to dominate its society and politics.

COMMUNIST A person who believes in communism, a political system in which all property is commonly owned by people and all wealth divided among them equally or according to their needs.

Sabarmati Ashram in Ahmedabad, India

DIVIDE AND RULE When a government encourages division between different groups so that they do not remain united to oppose it.

HARIJAN A Hindi word meaning "Children of God." A name given by Mahatma Gandhi to the group of people formerly called "untouchables."

HARTAL A Hindi word for going on strike against a government, employer, or any other authority.

HINDUISM The religion of the majority of people in India, based on a wide range of beliefs and traditions, gods and goddesses, and sacred texts. It evolved over centuries, with no single founder or holy book.

IMPERIALISM The policy of making a country stronger and richer by ruling or exercising control over other countries.

INDENTURED LABOR A system of servitude in which indebted people are bound to employers for a specified time, regardless of harsh conditions or meager pay.

INDIAN NATIONAL CONGRESS An Indian political party that was founded in 1885. It played a key role in the Indian freedom struggle, turning it into a mass movement under the leadership of Mahatma Gandhi.

INDUSTRIAL REVOLUTION The transition to a new manufacturing process based on machine-made, factory-based, and steam-powered manufacture of goods. It began in 18th-century England and spread across the world. The invention of the steam engine spurred the development of steam boats, railroad locomotives, and automobiles.

followers, called Muslims, believe only one God, Allah, and follow their ly book, the *Quran*.

HILAFAT A political movement in hich Muslims protested against the olishment of the Islamic Caliphate d loss of Caliph's powers after WWI.

NIGHTHOOD A title given to a man by e British monarch for his achievements his service to his country.

SHATRIYA One of the four broad oupings, or *varna*, that make up e traditional Indian caste system. e Kshatriya group includes the ling and warrior class.

AHATMA A Sanskrit word for reat soul"; the title given to ohandas Gandhi to acknowledge s saintly qualities.

ATUROPATHY system of aying healthy d treating nesses by tural means ch as diet ntrol, massage, d the use of ter and sunlight.

Slave chains

AX BRITANNICA tin for "British Peace," imposed the British Empire upon hostile tions in the 19th century.

OORNA SWARAJ A Hindi phrase eaning "total independence."

RINCELY STATES The term used by e British rulers for Indian kingdoms.

ROTECTORATE An autonomous territory der the military protection of a stronger untry but not directly ruled by it.

ACISM The belief that some people e inferior to others because of their in color, leading to prejudice and scrimination against them.

EVOLUTION A thorough change in litical, social, or economic systems, king place over a short period of time.

---

that don't flush.

SCHEDULED CASTES The official term used to describe the castes formerly called "untouchables" in India.

SEDITION The political act of inciting people to rebel against a government.

SEPARATE ELECTORATES A system of elections in which people of a certain community vote separately for their own representatives.

SHUDRA One of the four social groups, or *varna*, that make up the traditional Indian caste system. The Shudra group includes manual laborers and is deemed the lowest in the traditional Indian caste hierarchy.

SLAVERY A system in which people were captured and forced to do unpaid labor for those belonging to powerful social groups or nations. Slaves were viewed as the property of their masters.

SOCIALISM A political and economic system in which important economic resources, such as farms and industries, are owned and managed by the government in the name of the people.

SWADESHI A Hindi word for "of own country," referring to products made domestically.

SWARAJ A Hindi word for "self-rule" or "home rule."

SWASTIKA An ancient symbol of good fortune in the Indian subcontinent, as well as in Europe. A modified version was adopted and its meaning perverted by Adolf Hitler's Nazi Party.

SUFFRAGETTES Female activists who struggled for women's right to vote in the UK and the US during the late 19th and early 20th centuries.

---

scavenging, considered "impure" in the Indian caste system and fell outside the caste society.

Madame Blavatsky

VAISHNAVA A person belonging to a sect of Hinduism devoted to the worship of Lord Vishnu and his 10 incarnations.

VAISHYA One of the four broad social groups, or *varna*, that make up the Indian caste system. The Vaishya group includes traders and agriculturalists.

VARNA The traditional Indian system of organizing society into four hereditary groups or castes, based on the work people do. The four *varna* are Brahmins (priests and scholars), Kshatriyas (rulers and warriors), Vaishyas (merchants and farmers), and Shudras (laborers).

WHITE MAN'S BURDEN A 19th-century concept stating that white Europeans were the most civilized race and as such obliged to teach civilization to inferior races. It was popularized in a Rudyard Kipling poem of the same name.

Dedicated to THE WOMEN'S SOCIAL AND POLITICAL UNION.

VOTES FOR WOMEN W.S.P.U.

THE MARCH OF THE WOMEN
(Popular Edition in F. To be sung in Unison)
By **ETHEL SMYTH**, Mus.Doc.
Price: One Shilling & Sixpence net.
To be had of THE WOMAN'S PRESS 156 Charing Cross Rd London W.C. and BREITKOPF & HÄRTEL 54 & Marlborough St London W.

The songsheet of the anthem of the suffragettes, 1911

Index

Acknowledgments

Dorling Kindersley would like to thank: Alka Thakur and Kingshuk Ghoshal for proofreading; Rupa Rao for editorial assistance; Deep Shikha Walia for design assistance; Rakesh Khundongbam for illustrations, and Vikas Kanchan for index.

Special thanks to Dr. Mani Mala and other staff members of Gandhi Smriti and Darshan Samiti for allowing us to use images from their library.

The publisher would like to thank the following for their kind permission to reproduce their photographs:

(Key: a-above; b-below/bottom; c-center; f-far; l-left; r-right; t-top)

2 Alamy Images: Interfoto (crb); Dinodia Photos (c); Oleksiy Maksymenko (br). Mullock's Auctioneers: (c/prayer beads). Gandhi Smriti and Darshan Samiti: Deepak Aggarwal (bl). Getty Images: British Library / Robana / Hulton Fine Art Collection (cb); Henry Guttman / Hulton Archive (tl). www.ushaseejarim.com: Usha Seejarim, 2006 (tr). 3 Alamy Images: Interfoto (tl). Gandhi Smriti and Darshan Samiti: Deepak Aggarwal (tr). Getty Images: Don Emmert (tr). 4 Corbis: Heritage Images (bl). Dorling Kindersley: Ivy Roy (tr). Dreamstime.com: Fredwellman (r). Gandhi Smriti and Darshan Samiti: (br); Deepak Aggarwal (cl). Getty Images: WIN-Initiative (bc). Vishnu Menon (r). 5 Gina Rohekar: From the collection of Sherry Rohekar (tr). 6 Alamy Images: Oleksiy Maksymenko (cl). 6-7 Corbis: Hulton-Deutsch Collection. 7 Getty Images: Imagno / Hulton Archive (c); Mondadori (r). 8 Alamy Images: The Art Gallery Collection (tl). Getty Images: Royal Geographical Society, London (clb). 8-9 Dorling Kindersley: The Science Museum, London (b). 9 Corbis: (r). Getty Images: Time & Life Pictures (cr). 10 Alamy Images: Dinodia Photos (br). Gandhi Smriti and Darshan Samiti: (tl). 11 Alamy Images: Dinodia Photos (bl). Dorling Kindersley: Romi Chakraborty (tl). Gandhi Smriti and Darshan Samiti: (tl). Getty Images: Mondadori (tr). Koshur Saal: Chandramukhi Ganju (cb). 12-13 Corbis: Hulton-Deutsch Collection (b). 12 Getty Images: Henry Guttman / Hulton Archive (r). 13 Getty Images: London Stereoscopic Company / Hulton Archive (tr). 14 Gandhi Smriti and Darshan Samiti: Deepak Aggarwal (cr). Mary Evans Picture Library: (bl). 14-15 Corbis: Jon Hrusa. 15 Alamy Images: Dinodia Photos (br). Documentation Centre (Ukzn): (tl). Gandhi Smriti and Darshan Samiti: (tr). 16 Alamy Images: Classic Image (bl); Interfoto (tl). The Bridgeman Art Library: Private Collection (c). 16-17 Alamy Images: Dinodia Photos (b). 17 Documentation Centre (Ukzn): (tl/Indian pass, tl/Industrial service, tl/Service contract). Dreamstime.com: Artem Khabeev (tl/hand). Gandhi Smriti and Darshan Samiti: (tr). www.ushaseejarim.com: Usha Seejarim, 2006 (tr). 18 Fotolia: rook76 (br). 18-19 Corbis: Hulton-Deutsch Collection. 19 akg-images: R. u. S. Michaud (br). Alamy Images: RGB Ventures LLC dba SuperStock (tr). Corbis: Heritage Images (c). Gandhi Smriti and Darshan Samiti: (cla). Getty Images: David Evans / National Geographic (clb). 20 Alamy Images: North Wind Picture Archives (b). Dreamstime.com: Eyeblink (c/Black pepper). Fotolia: Grecaud Paul (cr). Getty Images: British Library / Robana / Hulton Fine Art Collection (t). 21 Dorling Kindersley: National Railway Museum, New Dehli (b). Getty Images: Hulton Archive (cr); British Library / Robana / Hulton Fine Art Collection (t). Mary Evans Picture Library: (cb). 22 Getty Images: DEA / G. Dagli Orti (cl). 22-23 Gina Rohekar: From the collection of Sherry Rohekar. 23 Gandhi Smriti and Darshan Samiti: (tr). Wikipedia: Uma Dhupelia-Mesthrie / Isabel Hofmeyr (cb). 24 Dreamstime.com: Fredwellman (bl). Gandhi Smriti and Darshan Samiti: (cl). 24-25 Alamy Images: Dinodia Photos (b). 25 Alamy Images: Dinodia Photos (cr); Robert Harding Picture Library Ltd (br); Seapix (br). Corbis: Rykoff Collection (r). 26 Alamy Images: Dinodia Photos (br). Getty Images: WIN-Initiative (tr). 26-27 Alamy Images: Maurice Joseph (b). Getty Images: Don Emmert (cal). 27 Alamy Images: Dinodia Photos (crb). 28 akg-images: Archiv Peter Rühe (tl). Alamy Images: Dinodia Photos (bl). 28-29 Alamy Images: Dinodia Photos. 29 Gandhi Smriti and Darshan Samiti: (tl, c, tr). Getty Images: Wallace Kirkland / TIME

& LIFE Images (bl). 30 akg-images: Archiv Peter Rühe (bl). Nehru Memorial Museum & Library: (tl). 30-31 Alamy Images: Dinodia Photos. 31 akg-images: Yvan Travert (tr). Corbis: Bettmann (br). The University of Warwick: Iron and Steel Trades Confederation (ISTC), Modern Records Centre (cb). 32 Dreamstime.com: Engin Korkmaz (tl). 32-33 Getty Images: Topical Press Agency / Hulton Archive. 33 Alamy Images: Dinodia Photos (tr). Corbis: Bettmann (br). 34 Alamy Images: Interfoto (tl). 34-35 Getty Images: Rolls Press / Popperfoto. 35 Gandhi Smriti and Darshan Samiti: (tl/Gandhi with charkha). Getty Images: Keren Su / China Span (tl). Manoj Kumar: (tr). 36-37 Alamy Images: Dinodia Photos (t). Corbis: Jim Craigmyle (Background). Dreamstime.com: R. Gino Santa Maria (b/Open book). Gandhi Smriti and Darshan Samiti: Deepak Aggarwal (c). 36 Dreamstime.com: Empire331 (crb); Plmrue (bc); R. Gino Santa Maria (bc/3 books). Getty Images: Universal Images Group (cl). 37 Corbis: Bettmann (tl); Hulton-Deutsch Collection (r). 38 R.K. Laxman: (r). 38-39 Alamy Images: Dinodia Photos. 39 Gandhi Smriti and Darshan Samiti: (tr). Getty Images: Raveendran / AFP (cr); Margaret Bourke-White / Time & Life Pictures (c). Vishnu Menon: (tl). 40 Alamy Images: Dinodia Photos (b). Corbis: Bettmann (tl). 41 Alamy Images: Dinodia Photos (cl). Corbis: Bettmann (tl). Gandhi Smriti and Darshan Samiti: (bl). Getty Images: Margaret Bourke-White / Time & Life Pictures (tr); March Of Time / Time & Life Pictures (bc). 42 Corbis: Dinodia (cr). 43 akg-images: Archiv Peter Rühe (tl). Alamy Images: Interfoto (cb); Travelib prime (tr); DIZ Muenchen GmbH, Sueddeutsche Zeitung Photo (cl). Getty Images: Mondadori / Autographic (Letter); Manan Vatsyayana / AFP (br). 44 Alamy Images: Dinodia Photos (r). 44-45 Dr. Bhavin Patel. 45 Corbis: Getty Images: UniversalImagesGroup (tr). Mary Evans Picture Library: John Frost Newspapers (cr). 46 Getty Images: Keystone-France (cl). 46-47 Corbis: Hulton-Deutsch Collection. 47 Getty Images: PjrStudio (bl). Corbis: CinemaPhoto (cr). 48 Corbis: Heritage Images (bl). 48-49 Corbis: Hulton-Deutsch Collection. 49 Alamy Images: Interfoto (r). Corbis: Bettmann (b). 50 akg-images: Archiv Peter Rühe (clb). Corbis: Hulton-Deutsch Collection (tl). 50-51 Dorling Kindersley: Priyanka Thakur (tr). 51 Corbis: Bettmann (tr); Dinodia (tl). 52-53 Getty Images: Keystone-France (tl). 52 Getty Images: Popperfoto (cl). 53 Corbis: Hulton-Deutsch Collection (tl). Gandhi Smriti and Darshan Samiti: (tr). 54-55 Corbis: Bettmann. 54 Getty Images: Margaret Bourke-White / Time & Life Pictures (tl). 55 Corbis: Bettmann (tr). Getty Images: Dinodia Photos (br). 56 Corbis: (tl). Getty Images: Keystone / Hulton Archive (bl). 56-57 Corbis: Bettmann. Dreamstime.com: Dmitry Rukhlenko (t). 57 Corbis: Raminder Pal Singh / epa (br). Getty Images: Hulton Archive (tr). 58-59 Gandhi Smriti and Darshan Samiti. 59 Corbis: Bettmann (bl). Getty Images: Fox Photos / Hulton Archive (r). Nehru Memorial Museum & Library: (bc). 60 Corbis: Radu Sigheti / X00255 / Reuters (cl). Getty Images: Gamma-Keystone (clb). 60-61 Corbis: Bettmann. 61 Corbis: Rick Friedman / Pool (br); Pete Marovich (cl). Getty Images: Frank Barratt / Hulton Archive (tr). 62 Alamy Images: PjrStudio (c). Corbis: Bob Adelman (clb). Getty Images: New York Daily News Archive (tl). 62-63 Corbis: Bettmann. 63 Corbis: Osman Orsal (br). Getty Images: Travel Ink / Gallo Images (cr). 64 Getty Images: Underwood Archives / Archive Photos (tc); British Library / Robana / Hulton Fine Art Collection (c). 64-65 Corbis: Brandon Tabiolo / Design Pics. 65 Corbis: Hulton-Deutsch Collection (cb); A.J. Historical (bl). Gandhi Smriti and Darshan Samiti: Deepak Aggarwal (tr). Getty Images: Science & Society Picture Library (tr). Jamie Tully: (cl). 66 Gandhi Smriti and Darshan Samiti: (tl); Deepak Aggarwal (c). Getty Images: NBCUniversal (bl). 66-67 Corbis: Brandon Tabiolo / Design Pics. Gandhi Smriti and Darshan Samiti: Deepak Aggarwal. 67 Alamy Images: Arnel Manalang (br); SCPhotos (tl). 70-71 Corbis: Brandon Tabiolo / Design Pics. 70 Dinudey Baidya: (b). Getty Images: Popperfoto (cl). Gina Rohekar: From the collection of Sherry Rohekar (tc). 71 Corbis: Hulton-Deutsch Collection (tr); Godong / Robert Harding World Imagery (tl); Heritage Images (br). Dorling Kindersley: Royal Geographical Society, London (cl).

Jacket images: Front: Alamy Images: Interfoto c/ (South Africa medal), Oleksiy Maksymenko cl/ (Three monkeys), Dinodia Photos r, cl; Mullock's Auctioneers: c/ (Prayer beads). Dorling Kindersley: Ivy Roy c/ (Sign on the house); Dreamstime.com: Empire331 c/ (Ink and pen), Fredwellman ca, Engin Korkmaz c/ (Ottoman symbol); Gandhi Smriti and Darshan Samiti: Deepak Aggarwal c, bl/ (Charkha); Getty Images: Don Emmert cb, WIN-Initiative c/ (Wooden sandals); www.ushaseejarim.com: Usha Seejarim, 2006 clb; Back: Gandhi Smriti and Darshan Samiti: l

All other images © Dorling Kindersley
For further information see: www.dkimages.com